GANGS
FROM THE STREETS TO SOCIAL MEDIA

By Anna Collins

Portions of this book originally appeared in *Gangs* by Jenny MacKay.

LUCENT PRESS

Published in 2020 by
Lucent Press, an Imprint of Greenhaven Publishing, LLC
353 3rd Avenue
Suite 255
New York, NY 10010

Designer: Deanna Paternostro
Editor: Jennifer Lomardo

Cataloging-in-Publication Data

Names: Collins, Anna.
Title: Gangs: from the streets to social media / Anna Collins.
Description: New York : Lucent Press, 2020. | Series: Hot topics | Includes index.
Identifiers: ISBN 9781534567559 (pbk.) | ISBN 9781534566972 (library bound) | ISBN 9781534567566 (ebook)
Subjects: LCSH: Gangs–United States–Juvenile literature. | Gang members–United States--Juvenile literature. | Juvenile delinquency–United States–Prevention–Juvenile literature.
Classification: LCC HV6439.U5 C65 2020 | DDC 364.106'60973–dc23

Printed in the United States of America

CPSIA compliance information: Batch #BS19KL: For further information contact Greenhaven Publishing LLC, New York, New York at 1-844-317-7404.

Please visit our website, www.greenhavenpublishing.com. For a free color catalog of all our high-quality books, call toll free 1-844-317-7404 or fax 1-844-317-7405.

CONTENTS

FOREWORD 4

INTRODUCTION 6
What Is a Gang?

CHAPTER 1 10
The Rise of Gangs in the United States

CHAPTER 2 23
Underlying Issues

CHAPTER 3 40
The Gang Lifestyle

CHAPTER 4 52
Promoting and Recruiting

CHAPTER 5 68
Solving the Problem

NOTES 85

DISCUSSION QUESTIONS 93

ORGANIZATIONS TO CONTACT 95

FOR MORE INFORMATION 97

INDEX 99

PICTURE CREDITS 103

ABOUT THE AUTHOR 104

Adolescence is a time when many people begin to take notice of the world around them. News channels, blogs, and talk radio shows are constantly promoting one view or another; very few are unbiased. Young people also hear conflicting information from parents, friends, teachers, and acquaintances. Often, they will hear only one side of an issue or be given flawed information. People who are trying to support a particular viewpoint may cite inaccurate facts and statistics on their blogs, and news programs present many conflicting views of important issues in our society. In a world where it seems everyone has a platform to share their thoughts, it can be difficult to find unbiased, accurate information about important issues.

It is not only facts that are important. In blog posts, in comments on online videos, and on talk shows, people will share opinions that are not necessarily true or false, but can still have a strong impact. For example, many young people struggle with their body image. Seeing or hearing negative comments about particular body types online can have a huge effect on the way someone views themselves and may lead to depression and anxiety. Although it is important not to keep information hidden from young people under the guise of protecting them, it is equally important to offer encouragement on issues that affect their mental health.

The titles in the Hot Topics series provide readers with different viewpoints on important issues in today's society. Many of these issues, such as gang violence and gun control laws, are of immediate concern to young people. This series aims to give readers factual context on these crucial topics in a way that lets them form their own opinions. The facts presented throughout also serve to empower readers to help themselves or support people they know who are struggling with many of the challenges adolescents face today. Although negative viewpoints are not ignored or downplayed, this series allows young people to see that the challenges they face are not insurmountable. As increasing numbers of young adults join political debates, especially regarding gun violence, learning the facts as well as the views of others will help them decide where they stand—and understand what they are fighting for.

Quotes encompassing all viewpoints are presented and cited so readers can trace them back to their original source, verifying for themselves whether the information comes from a reputable place. Additional books and websites are listed, giving readers a starting point from which to continue their own research. Chapter questions encourage discussion, allowing young people to hear and understand their classmates' points of view as they further solidify their own. Full-color photographs and enlightening charts provide a deeper understanding of the topics at hand. All of these features augment the informative text, helping young people understand the world they live in and formulate their own opinions concerning the best way they can improve it.

What Is a Gang?

The term "gang" has very negative associations in today's society, but this was not always the case. In the past, it simply referred to a group, and even today it can still be used in this sense; as the *Chicago Tribune* pointed out, "'The whole gang's here!' is rarely meant as a plea for police protection."[1] However, over time, "gang" has also come to mean a group of people who participate in illegal or violent activity.

Gangs create legal and social issues all across the United States as well as in other parts of the world—even in places people might not expect, such as Sweden and Japan. Gangs are often presented by the media as a modern problem; however, they have existed for centuries. In the 2016 presidential election, they became a major political topic when Republican candidate Donald Trump stated that he wanted to build a wall between the United States and Mexico to stop gang members and other criminals from moving between the two countries. The political focus on gangs continued through 2018, as fears about a gang called MS-13, which has a strong hold on certain Latin American countries, surged. Public opinion has been fiercely divided: Some believe slowing or stopping immigration is necessary to prevent the United States from taking in gang members, while others say such measures only hurt nonviolent immigrants. Additionally, experts say gangs are not created out of the stresses of immigration alone, nor are immigrant groups the only population from which gangs draw their members. Gangs form among every ethnic group and can be found in most, if not all, countries.

Why Do People Join Gangs?

Sociologists, law enforcement agencies, youth specialists, and others who study gangs have learned that gangs seem to arise in situations where people feel left out of mainstream society and have lost a sense of hope for the future. Gangs provide them with a sense of belonging and a feeling that they are part of something important. In many cases, they also provide a sense of security; they tend to form in places where people feel unsafe, such as prisons or neighborhoods with a high rate of violence. Unfortunately, the presence of gangs in these places makes them even more unsafe, as rival gangs tend to fight, hurting each other as well as innocent bystanders. In such situations, people tend to feel that joining a gang is a requirement; otherwise, they will be targeted by all rival gangs in the area.

Gangs are also common in poorer areas because they promise their members the opportunity to make a lot of money through criminal activity such as dealing drugs, selling weapons, and stealing. Additionally, these poorer areas offer very little in the way of entertainment, especially to young adults. Gangs offer teens the opportunity to hang out and entertain each other—often in ways that involve illegal activity, such as committing vandalism and doing drugs.

According to the National Gang Center—an organization that researches gangs and educates people about the realities of gangs as well as how to reduce their influence—the number of gangs in the United States declined steadily from 1996 to 2003, then began to rise again. Since gangs frequently participate in illegal activity, not all of them advertise their presence, so hard data is difficult to come by. However, as of 2012—the most recent year for which estimates are available—there were about 30,000 gangs in the country, which "represents a 15 percent increase from 2006 and is the highest annual estimate since 1996."[2] Although the media frequently focuses on gangs involving people of color, much of the increase is coming from white gangs.

Gang crime, gang violence, and their ever-expanding size and numbers are important issues for community leaders,

police departments, and citizens concerned about the safety
and well-being of their neighborhoods. However, statistics
alone cannot give an accurate picture of gangs. People who live
near them, study them, or belong to one often find different
truths about gangs than what statistics may lead the general
public to believe. Although many gangs operate as criminal
enterprises with a long track record of drug use and reckless
violence, most of the people who belong to them also consider gangs to be caring families, reliable employers, and loyal
protectors—at least when they first join.

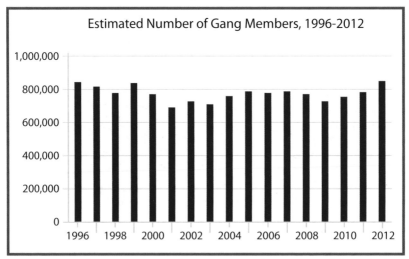

The number of gang members in the United States has risen and fallen over the
years, but never to less than 600,000, as this information from the National Gang
Center shows.

Additionally, although gangs have become a common and
negative topic in the media in recent decades, gangs also enjoy
great popularity in pop culture, including movies, TV shows,
and songs. Gangs are often violent, mysterious, and poorly un-
derstood by mainstream society, but American culture glorifies
them and sometimes portrays them as heroic enterprises.

Despite their sometimes glorified image, gangs can have very
serious consequences for society. The gang culture is primarily
one of crime, drug abuse, deadly violence, poverty, run-down
neighborhoods, and the destruction of gang members' futures,
since gang members have a high risk of being either killed on

the streets by rival gangs or sent to prison for committing gang-related crimes. Knowing why and how gangs form, what triggers their violent or criminal behaviors, and why new members join them despite the risks to their personal safety and freedom could help researchers and communities address gang-related problems. Police forces and civic leaders in communities across America are coming together to search for ways to reduce gang violence and crime and encourage people not to join gangs.

Because gangs commit crimes, their members
experience a high risk of ending up in prison.

Although myths and mysteries have surrounded gangs for hundreds of years, gang violence and crime are very real, and so are the socioeconomic factors that most experts say give rise to gangs in so many different communities around the world. To their members, gangs are important social institutions. The rest of society cannot treat them simply as things to be feared, dreaded, and removed from the world. Instead, people must work to separate fiction about gangs from the realities of gang life and understand that the people who join them are real people with real concerns. Understanding the gang phenomenon is a crucial step in responding to what many see as the growing crisis of gangs. They are an issue of concern as well as controversy across the United States and the rest of the world.

CHAPTER 1

The Rise of Gangs in the United States

Gangs are not unique to the United States, but few other countries glorify them the way some Americans do. The lures of power and money have made many people overlook some of the terrible deeds gang members commit. Some rap songs, in particular, have lyrics that describe how good it feels to be in a gang. Songs such as Scarface's "Diary of a Madman" and the Geto Boys' "Straight Gangstaism," as well as movies such as *Straight Outta Compton*, show gang membership as something that makes a person rich, powerful, and cool. In reality, however, joining a gang generally has a huge negative influence on a person's life.

Poverty, fear, lack of opportunities, and the absence of positive adult guidance have always been factors at the heart of American gangs. Combined with a feeling of displacement, either because of immigration or an environment of social inequality, these are ingredients for the formation of gangs. Gangs have existed throughout American history, generally deep within cities but always on the outskirts of mainstream, or typical, society. They have grown during certain periods of history, while at other times, their populations have decreased. Gangs have consisted of members of different ages and ethnicities and have spoken many different languages over the years. They have been blamed for many of society's problems; they have been publicized, too, as products of those problems. Through it all, gangs have been a constant phenomenon in American history.

FALSE CLAIMS

"Some [gangs] have even gone so far as to claim that they were formed to protect the community. The harsh reality is that gangs have been established to prey on the poorest community members who tend to be the most vulnerable and invisible in our society. Have you ever heard of a gang establishing an after-school tutoring program or a scholarship program from drug proceeds [profits]?"

—Randy Jurado Ertll, who grew up in south Los Angeles, California, where gang activity is high

Randy Jurado Ertll, "Hollywood Too Often Glorifies the Gangster Life: Guest Commentary," *San Gabriel Valley Tribune*, last updated August 30, 2017. www.sgvtribune.com/2015/08/14/hollywood-too-often-glorifies-the-gangster-life-guest-commentary/.

Early History

Criminal gangs first began to grow in U.S. cities in the 1800s. It was a time of heavy immigration, when thousands of people from European countries came to the United States in search of a better way of life. Irish, Italian, and Jewish immigrants flocked to the United States, but instead of the American dream of wealth and equality that many were seeking, they instead found racism, poverty, and an inner-city environment that was overcrowded, hostile, and dangerous. They began to form gangs that fit the modern definition well: They had names, they had distinct territories within cities such as New York City, and violent crime became a lifestyle for them.

To understand why gangs seemed to form so readily among immigrants in the 1800s, sociologists have examined the way they lived. Nineteenth-century gangs, in large part, seem to have been a widespread and natural human response to intolerable living conditions. Gangs developed among all the major groups of immigrants coming to the United States in the 19th century, but most famously among the Irish and Italians. These immigrants lived in extremely filthy, crowded places. Some slept 10 to a room in inner-city slum dwellings that lacked running

Shown here are members of the Short Tail gang, who were known to kill and steal on the Lower East Side of New York City in the late 1800s.

water and flushing toilets. Most immigrants were uneducated and not qualified for high-paying jobs. For Italians, finding work was even more difficult because many did not yet speak English. Most of the jobs immigrants could find involved long hours of hard work for very little pay—sometimes not even enough to pay for housing and food.

Making matters worse, many Americans did not like the immigrant groups that were arriving in growing numbers in the 1800s. They developed demeaning, or humiliating, ethnic names for immigrants, and they resisted allowing immigrants into mainstream American neighborhoods, jobs, or ways of life. The late journalist David Kales described how Americans in Boston, Massachusetts, treated Irish immigrants in the early 1800s. They would "rampage through Irish neighborhoods, where they shouted racial slurs, beat up passersby, [and] smashed windows,"[3] he wrote. The Italians fared no better. They too lived in slums, were disliked by other Americans, held mostly unskilled labor jobs, and lived in fear of being evicted by cruel landlords if they could not pay their rent.

Hostile surroundings and the need for self-protection drove immigrants in America's cities to unite within their own nationality and to hate and fear other ethnic groups. Additionally, they were coming with their own biases, formed in the countries they had previously lived in. They laid claim to particular neighborhoods of their cities and were wary of any intruders or strangers. Many historians and sociologists say that the violent,

The Sicilian Mafia

Immigration is not the only factor leading to the formation of gangs. In general, any area where people feel ignored by society and desperate to meet their basic needs is vulnerable to gang formation. While Italians were forming the Mafia crime organization in the United States in the 19th century, Italians living in Sicily were doing the same thing. The two organizations share a name—both call themselves the Mafia—and some traditions, but they are not the same group. According to the History Channel, Sicily was the victim of frequent attacks by invaders, so "Sicilians banded together in groups to protect themselves and carry out their own justice."[1] However, this eventually turned into illegal activities that threatened others, such as demanding what they called "protection money": They claimed to be protecting landowners in exchange for payment, but in reality, they were implying that they would attack the landowners if they did not pay the Mafia.

In the 1870s, after Sicily had become part of Italy, the Italian government "asked Sicilian Mafia clans to help them by going after dangerous, independent criminal bands; in exchange, officials would look the other way as the Mafia continued its protection shakedowns of landowners."[2] This was meant to be a temporary measure until the government could establish better control, but it allowed the Mafia so much freedom that it became impossible to uproot. Even the Catholic Church became involved, using the Mafia to protect its own lands and power. The Sicilian Mafia is nowhere near as powerful today as it was in the past, but it is still operating today.

1. History.com Staff, "Origins of the Mafia," the History Channel, accessed on August 2, 2018. www.history.com/topics/origins-of-the-mafia.
2. History.com Staff, "Origins of the Mafia."

territorial nature of immigrant groups was a response to the racism and impoverished conditions of the overcrowded cities they lived in. "Youth and other community violence are a function of civil unrest and upheaval," wrote humanities researcher

Steven David Valdivia. "As social conditions worsen in an area, violence increases."[4]

Branching off into distinct territories within cities may have been a survival technique for ethnic groups who felt threatened and vulnerable, but it also created the perfect environment for criminal street gangs. As immigrants in cities such as New York City and Chicago, Illinois, laid claim to particular neighborhoods, they also invented names for themselves and began turning to crime as a way to earn extra money and gain a sense of power in an American society that had shunned them. Adding to the problem was the orphaned nature of immigrants. Many were young men who had set out on their own to start a new life in the United States; others had come to the country with their families but were left alone and unsupervised while their parents worked long hours at low-paying jobs to make ends meet.

At first, when these young men joined one another and formed some of the first American gangs—such as the Whyos, a mostly Irish gang in New York City in the late 1860s—they were separate from and even ignored by the rest of American society. Gang territories, or turfs, were considered bad parts of town and were completely avoided by outsiders, even by law enforcement officers. "Criminals and gang members had little to fear from the police as long as they stuck to their own neighborhoods,"[5] wrote Thomas A. Reppetto, former president of the New York City Crime Commission. Eventually, however, the gang population grew so large and its criminal ways so powerful that gang crime began to spill over into surrounding communities. No longer seen as a mere product of the social problems of the times, gangs also became a significant cause of social conflict and upheaval in America by the early 1900s.

Problems Caused by Gangs

By 1910, according to Reppetto, the city of New York had become "a metropolis where nearly three-quarters of the inhabitants were either immigrants or the children of immigrants."[6] One particular block of Manhattan known as the Five Points became home to some of America's first organized criminal gangs. Gangs such as the Dead Rabbits, the Plug Uglies, and the Bowery Boys ran gambling rings and brutally fought to protect their turf from other gangs. Some were made up of people of a particular ethnicity; for example, the Dead Rabbits were an Irish gang. Others were made up of immigrants who had been living in the United States for longer than the new arrivals. These were called nativist gangs because they believed "that America belonged solely to the white men who'd colonized it."[7] Fistfights, knife fights, and shootouts between gangs plagued the streets of New York City. Citizens who were not in gangs demanded that something be done. Police attempted to crack down on the problem, but some powerful members of the mainstream culture began to see gangs as a potential advantage.

Even in the 1800s, gang wars were disruptive and dangerous. Shown here is an 1850s illustration of a fight between the Dead Rabbits and the Bowery Boys.

Politicians, particularly those in big cities such as New York City and Chicago, recognized that as gangs grew in size and power, they could pressure people to vote for one politician over another and even scare voters away from the polls to prevent them from casting ballots for certain candidates. The 1900s brought about the start of a political era in which politicians, police, and gang leaders began forming corrupt alliances. Some gangs had grown wealthy from crime and powerful because of their violent actions. They paid off police to avoid arrest and called in favors from politicians who used gangs' power to get elected. Once these politicians were in office, they protected gangs from police investigation. Gangs grew in size, wealth, political connections, and influence until they ruled America's largest cities in the first few decades of the 1900s. By that time, gangs were seen as agents of terror, crime, and corruption. They had grown so large and powerful that they were able to expand their activities and participate in crime on an even wider scale. This turned them from small gangs into large crime organizations.

In the 1920s, Prohibition—a government policy that banned the sale of alcohol—came into effect. Gangs, already well-established in city life and largely protected by corrupt police officers and politicians, stepped up to run the illegal alcohol trade. What came next was an era of gang-related crime, power, terror, and murder that rocked American society. This was when the deadliest and most notorious mobsters—among them Lucky Luciano, Dutch Schultz, Bugs Moran, and the infamous Al Capone—rose to power by achieving great wealth from the illegal alcohol trade. They used their money to bribe police officers and elected officials into ignoring their illegal activities. Anyone they could not bribe, they murdered. The violent tactics of these Prohibition-era gangs earned them brutal reputations that have contributed to the negative public opinion of—and the fascination with—gangs ever since.

New Gangs Arise

After Prohibition was repealed, or ended, in 1933, the U.S. government began a campaign to end political corruption, lock up crime bosses, and stamp out the menacing gang problem that for years had run wild in America. For a while, the crackdown on gangs seemed to work. However, although criminal organizations lost much of the power they had previously held, gangs could not be entirely eliminated. "Gang behavior and gang development tend to run in 'cycles,'" explained sociology professor Donald J. Shoemaker. "That is, gang membership seems to swing in cycles involving as much as five or ten years ... Efforts to curb, reduce, or prevent gang activity may reflect cyclical patterns of gang membership and behavioral patterns as much as the efforts of the gang prevention programs."[8]

The Yakuza and the Triads

Other countries also have a long history of gang activity that continues to this day. In Japan, for example, "the term yakuza can be used to refer to individual gangsters or criminals as well as to their organized groups and to Japanese organized crime in general."[1] Yakuza have secret rituals and detailed tattoos, and they engage in a variety of criminal activities, including gambling, drug and sex trafficking, and smuggling. They have been around in one form or another since the early 17th century, but they did not reach the height of their power until the early 1960s. According to *Encyclopedia Britannica*, "While their methods are often questionable, they have been known to perform charitable acts, such as donating and delivering supplies to earthquake victims."[2] Because of this as well as the portrayal of gangs in Western media, some Japanese people look up to them or see them as a way to control more disorganized crime.

The triads are another Asian gang organization with roots in the 17th century. Like the yakuza, they have special ceremonies and elaborate tattoos, and they came to the height of their power in the 1960s. At that time, there were about 60 triad groups in Hong Kong, and about 1 in 6 citizens were members.

Members of the yakuza get colorful Japanese-style tattoos to show that they belong to the gang.

The yakuza and triads also share characteristics with the Italian Mafia: a clear social hierarchy, or order, and strict codes of behavior. However, they are less well-known and discussed less often in popular media than the Mafia. For example, although a Chinese crime organization similar to the triads was featured in "The Blind Banker," a 2010 episode of the popular BBC show *Sherlock*, it was not identified by name. In contrast, entire movies and television shows, such as *The Godfather* and *The Sopranos*, have centered around the Mafia.

1. The Editors of *Encyclopedia Britannica*, "Yakuza: Japanese Organized Crime," *Encyclopedia Britannica*, last updated June 21, 2018. www.britannica.com/topic/yakuza.
2. The Editors of *Encyclopedia Britannica*, "Yakuza: Japanese Organized Crime."

By the 1950s and 1960s, American society had mostly come to terms with its Irish, Italian, and Jewish citizens, and European immigration had slowed considerably. However, cultural differences among Americans were far from over. New immigrants from Central and South America and Asia arrived in the United States and found much of the same cultural intolerance, poor living conditions, and lack of good jobs that had beset the immigrants of a century before. In response to these conditions, Latinx and Asian youths condensed in American cities in the mid-1900s and began to form new gangs. The Latin Kings, for example, a gang of Puerto Rican immigrants, formed in Chicago in the late 1950s. In the same decade, Mexican immigrants in Southern California formed a gang called Nuestra Familia (Our Family). Chinese immigrants, meanwhile, were banding together in cities such as San Francisco, California, where they formed the Joe Boys gang and the Yu Li gang in the 1960s. These and other gangs of immigrants were ancestors to some of the gangs that still exist in America today. They also provided evidence that immigrating to America created social conditions ripe for the formation of gangs, regardless of the ethnicity of the immigrants.

It was not just immigrants who felt displaced in American society. Black Americans, too, faced poverty, slums, racism, and inequality. The era of social activism against racial segregation during the 1950s and 1960s, known as the civil rights movement, was a time of extreme social conflict between black and white Americans. Many social and legal changes during this time brought black Americans and white Americans closer to social equality than ever before in history, but interracial violence and prejudice also made some black Americans feel as if they were being shoved to the edges of society. Many black gangs formed in America's cities during the 1950s and 1960s, such as the Vice Lords in Chicago, the Crips and the Bloods in Los Angeles, and the Black Spades in the Bronx of New York City. "The gang offered what [African American teenagers] absolutely needed to survive—protection, food and shelter, a sense of belonging, and self-esteem,"[9] said David Fattah, cofounder of the Philadelphia, Pennsylvania-based gang prevention program House of Umoja and a former gang member himself. Gangs that formed in the mid-1900s—among immigrants as well as African Americans—had many similarities to gangs of the 1800s. Some of the same gangs—and many newer groups like them—still exist today, and some former gang members have even gone on to become famous for other reasons. For example, rapper Cardi B has admitted that she joined the Bloods when she was 16. She had hinted at it previously in interviews as well as in some of her lyrics, but she said

Rapper Cardi B has spoken out about the fact that being in a gang is not the glamorous lifestyle it sometimes appears to be.

in 2018 that she finally felt secure enough her in fame to speak freely without hurting her chances of getting record deals. She has said she does not actively participate in the gang anymore but continues to reference it in her songs and on social media because she has already been doing it for so long. She explained, "it's not like, oh, you leave. You don't leave."[10]

White Gangs

Although everyone who lives in the United States—except for Native Americans—is an immigrant or descendant of immigrants, white people whose ancestors moved to the United States earlier have a tendency to look down on immigrants of any race who move there later. Because the Irish and Italians were white, they were eventually absorbed into mainstream American society, which means the media mainly focuses on gangs formed by people of color. However, the tendency of people to form gangs seems to be a natural human response to an environment of social struggles, regardless of their race or culture.

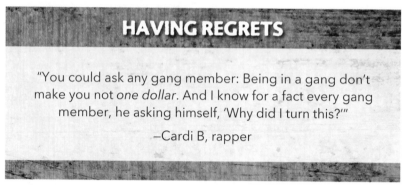

HAVING REGRETS

"You could ask any gang member: Being in a gang don't make you not *one dollar*. And I know for a fact every gang member, he asking himself, 'Why did I turn this?'"

—Cardi B, rapper

Quoted in Dee Lockett, "Cardi B Explains the Obvious Reason She's Always Repping the Bloods," *Vulture*, April 9, 2018. www.vulture.com/2018/04/cardi-b-confirms-why-shes-always-repping-the-bloods.html.

White gangs are not a recent trend. In addition to the nativist gangs in 19th-century New York, the Vietnam War created another period of intense social unrest in America that led to the rise of gangs. Many Americans were opposed to the war, so they protested against it and the soldiers who fought in it. Veterans who returned home from Vietnam often felt like outcasts, unwanted and disrespected by society. In the late 1970s, some Vietnam veterans purchased motorcycles and turned against mainstream America, vowing to live on the outskirts of society. They gave rise to multiple outlaw motorcycle, or biker, gangs, including the Bandidos, the Outlaws, and the Hells Angels, all of which still exist today. Outlaw motorcycle gangs consist mainly of older white men and are a violent social problem in many American cities. Not everyone who rides a motorcycle is in a biker gang, but they are so infamous that some people are automatically suspicious of anyone who has this type of vehicle—especially if they fit a person's mental image of someone who is in one of these gangs. Culturally different than the black, Latinx, and Asian gangs that also contribute to the modern gang population of America, biker gangs can nonetheless be traced back to the same kinds of social struggles and feelings of being outcasts that have been at the heart of gang formation in America throughout history.

Biker gangs are so infamous that some people have a prejudice against anyone who owns a motorcycle, even though not all motorcycle owners are in gangs.

Because white gangs are less likely to be featured in the news, people are less likely to think of white Americans as gang members, even though as many as 40 percent of self-identified American gang members are white. This extends even to the police; according to criminal law professor Babe Howell, police undercount the number of white gang members, placing their estimate at 10 to 14 percent. Because of this, white gang members are less likely to be punished by police when they are caught. Many white people are unaware of the privilege they have in today's society; they tend to have the belief that anyone who is caught doing something criminal will be appropriately punished, and that if someone goes unpunished, it is proof that they are innocent. In reality, the police sometimes turn a blind eye to white gang activity, focusing on the black and Latinx communities, where they believe the greater problem lies. As Howell explained, "Police see groups of young white people as individuals, each responsible for his or her own conduct, and hold young people of color in street gangs criminally liable for the conduct of their peers."[11]

Modern gangs continue to be a widespread social phenomenon in American society, and they are constantly growing in size and number. Attempts to define them, classify them, and react to them have given researchers interesting snapshots of the culture of modern gangs. Understanding that culture may be the key to addressing the social problems that gangs cause as well as the social problems that seem to cause them.

Underlying Issues

Gangs are considered a subculture, which is a cultural group that exists within a larger culture. Often, people in a subculture have different values than the main culture. This is true of gangs, which have their own rules, symbols, slang, and behavioral expectations. For example, while the larger culture of the country they live in tends to oppose violence, gangs embrace it as a way to punish people they perceive as enemies. Some gangs also use violence as a way to test their new members—for example, someone who expresses interest in joining a gang may be ordered to rob someone to prove their loyalty to the gang and willingness to follow orders. This is called an initiation. Rarely, they may also be ordered to kill someone at random; however, although there are many scary stories about this, there are very few known instances of it.

In an effort to find ways to prevent the spread of existing gangs and the formation of new ones, social scientists study gang populations, looking for trends in the way gangs form and the reasons why people join them. Throughout their long history, American gangs have seemed to follow similar patterns. In particular, they have been considered a stand-in for families when normal family ties fail, especially in the inner-city environment. However, the long-standing idea that gangs are strictly a "city problem" has proven dangerous to some rural communities, causing them to overlook gang activity in the mistaken belief that it could not possibly happen there.

Many people mistakenly think small towns do not have gangs—even some of the people who live in those towns believe this. Overlooking this problem means it is much harder to solve.

Gang members and researchers who study gangs say that gangs serve an important social purpose for their members—they provide a sense of family, belonging, and cultural identity for members who have not found other ways to meet these basic human needs. Because most of them participate in illegal moneymaking activities—including smuggling immigrants over the border illegally, identity theft, and drug trafficking—they are also attractive to people who live in areas where there are few job opportunities and where high rates of poverty make it difficult for them to meet their basic needs.

Gangs and Race

Many people think of gangs as an issue that mainly affects people of color. While it is true that common cultural experiences, language, and living near one another can build a foundation for ethnic gangs, they do not, in themselves, create gangs. Other social factors are almost always present when gangs form. In particular, the experience of hostility or discrimination from different ethnic groups is believed to lead to the development of gangs as a way for members to stand up for themselves. Part of the process of gang formation, according to criminologists Malcolm W. Klein and Cheryl L. Maxson, "includes the gang members' coming to view themselves as the victims of oppression, the unfair targets of racism, inequality, and suppression."[12] Since black and Latinx people deal with far more poverty and racism than people of most other ethnicities, they are at a higher risk for joining gangs. Native Americans also deal with high levels of racism and poverty, but their population is smaller, so they are frequently ignored by the media and researchers alike and have even less access to resources than people of any other race. There are Native American gangs, but there is little recorded data about them. According to the National Gang Center, the most recent police statistics available indicate that about 46 percent of gang members are Latinx, 35 percent are black, more than 11 percent are white, and all remaining races and ethnicities make up the remainder. However, these statistics may not be entirely accurate, as Babe Howell noted. The association of gang members with black and Latinx men is so strong that many black and Latinx men who have never been in gangs or done anything illegal are feared, suspected, and targeted by police.

LOSS CONTRIBUTES TO GANGS

"Native people have endured cultural alienation [isolation], the loss of their language and their land, the destruction of family and social structures. They've weathered [survived] the resulting social dysfunction. For some youth, gangs offer a shelter from those realities."

—Tristan Ahtone, journalist

Tristan Ahtone, "Boys in the Woods: A Saturday Night in White Earth with the Native Disciples," *Al Jazeera America*, January 23, 2015. projects.aljazeera.com/2015/01/native-gangs/native-disciples.html.

Immigration is frequently blamed for the rise of gangs in the United States. One of the most frequently-discussed gangs as of 2019 is called Mara Salvatrucha, more commonly known as MS-13. It was formed in Los Angeles in the 1980s by children of immigrants from the Latin American country of El Salvador who felt discriminated against and threatened by the people in the neighborhoods around them. The gang then spread to Latin American countries such as El Salvador, Guatemala, and Honduras, where its members were able to gain a lot of control within the governments and have contributed to making those countries extremely unsafe. President Donald Trump and his administration have often used the gang as an example of why the United States needs stronger border protection and stricter immigration policies. Many of his supporters agree with him, but many of his opponents have pointed out several problems with his logic: Multiple studies have shown that there is no direct link between immigration and crime, while others have shown that immigration reduces crime; Trump has stated that increased protection will prevent MS-13 members from sneaking into the country, when in fact, they have been in the United States for years; and MS-13, while dangerous and violent, is neither the biggest nor the most dangerous gang in the United States. According to José Miguel Cruz, director of research in the Kimberly Green Latin American and Caribbean Center at Florida International University (FIU),

> *in pointing to MS-13 to try to scare Americans into harsh new immigration restrictions, Trump is overstating the danger the gang poses here in the United States. Worse, by using the gang to demonize all Latino immigrants, Trump is building inner-city walls that alienate communities and risk making criminal organizations more powerful, both here and overseas ...*
>
> *MS-13 in the United States does not rule cities as it does in Central America (though Trump claimed it does). It has no official national leadership structure here and does not collude [make deals with] corrupt politicians to win elections.*[13]

Cruz, who has been researching Central American gangs since 1996, stated that it was the U.S. government's unwillingness to address the underlying causes of gang membership, such as poverty and racism, that contributed to MS-13's rise both nationally and internationally. In the 1980s, he wrote, the

The Federal Response to Gangs

Americans' fears about gangs—especially international ones—have been growing since the early 2000s. These fears have been increased by the spread of false information. For instance, "Attorney General Jeff Sessions has called MS-13 the most brutal of the gangs driving the drug trade ... Really, experts have found the gang has barely any role in the international drug trade."[1]

Government officials have also vowed to pass laws that limit immigration, stating that they want to prevent gang members from sneaking into the country. Some people believe that MS-13 leaders try to get into the country by bringing in children and pretending to be a family that wants to settle in the United States. In reality, experts have found, this is not a common occurrence—"there have been fewer than 200 cases of false family claims [in 2018] ... and there is no indication that any of those cases involved MS-13."[2] MS-13 was founded in the United States and many of its members have grown up in the country, so there is no need for them to sneak in.

Another controversial immigration policy passed by the government is its decision to stop providing asylum to victims of gang violence, due to fears that gang members will pose as their own victims to get into the country. "Asylum" describes political protection for certain immigrants who are fleeing danger in their home countries. While refugees are people who apply to live in the United States before they leave their home country, people seeking asylum do so afterward. They come to the country before getting the proper permission, but once officials determine that they meet the criteria for asylum, they can begin applying for refugee status. Experts have said that since MS-13 members are already here and there are other, easier ways for them to get into the country, this policy will only hurt people who are trying to get away from gang violence in their home countries.

1. Hannah Dreier, "I've Been Reporting on MS-13 for a Year. Here Are the 5 Things Trump Gets Most Wrong," ProPublica, June 25, 2018. www.propublica.org/article/ms-13-immigration-facts-what-trump-administration-gets-wrong.

2. Dreier, "I've Been Reporting on MS-13 for a Year."

government started to crack down on gang activity, arresting people even for crimes that were not violent, such as smoking marijuana. This action was intended to make people avoid gangs for fear of being arrested, but in reality, it "was in the juvenile centers and prisons that local kids … interacted with hardened criminals and learned how to run a gang."[14] When these young men were released from jail and later deported back to Central America for having a criminal record, they "networked with and learned from vicious drug cartel members and corrupt authorities."[15] El Salvador and other countries tried the same zero-tolerance arrest approach instead of addressing social problems, with similarly bad results.

Many people believe gang membership is limited to people of color, but in truth, thousands of gang members around the world are white.

Only a fraction of all immigrants to America during any time period have actually become gang members. Most find other ways to cope with life in a new country. The stressful experience of moving to a new country clearly is not the only factor that contributes to the formation of gangs. Gangs do not arise based on race or national origin alone; white gangs and multiracial gangs are becoming increasingly common. Many white gangs believe that white people are superior to people of color. Some white supremacist gangs refer to themselves as skinheads because they shave off their hair, but not all white gang members are skinheads. In fact, not all white gang members are white supremacists. For example, the Simon City Royals—a gang with a large presence in southern states such as Mississippi and one of the country's oldest and largest white gangs—created an alliance with the Black Gangster Disciples in the 1970s and began admitting Latinx members shortly afterward. The white members of the Royals, who are proud to claim they are not racist, are viewed as enemies by some other white gangs, such as the Aryan Brotherhood, who believe the white Royals have betrayed their race by associating with people of color.

Most white gangs arise in poor, rural areas, where people tend to feel looked down on as "rednecks." Their members tend to have little hope of improving their financial or social status in the future and often blame others—especially minority cultures—for their underprivileged lifestyle. Those who are likely to join a gang also share other risk factors with inner-city teens, such as exposure to drugs, a desire for excitement, an absence of strong adult role models, and a desire for belonging. However, the media tends to focus much more on black and Latinx gang members as well as on violence in urban areas, giving the impression that white, rural gangs are far rarer than they actually are. This leads people to deny or ignore the problem, causing it to get worse. According to the Mississippi Association of Gang Investigators, 53 percent of known gang members in the state are white, but the only people prosecuted under the state's gang laws between 2010 and 2017 were black. Not only does this clouded view make it easier for white people to get away with criminal activities, it also prevents them from accessing anti-gang programs that are geared specifically toward people of color. Because race in and of itself has so little to do with why people join gangs, the National Institute of Justice recommends that "gang-joining prevention strategies should address common factors that cut across racial and ethnic lines, such as poverty and immigration, social isolation and discrimination, drug use, limited educational opportunities, and low parental monitoring."[16]

IGNORANCE IS HARMFUL

"The world should know there are whites struggling in hoods as well as any other race, and more often than not those kids become gang members or drug addicts ... How can you help [with a problem] if you don't recognize it's there?"

—Benny Ivey, former Simon City Royals member

Quoted in Donna Ladd, "Dangerous, Growing, yet Unnoticed: The Rise of America's White Gangs," *Guardian*, April 5, 2018. www.theguardian.com/society/2018/apr/05/white-gangs-rise-simon-city-royals-mississippi-chicago.

Targeting Young People

Most people are young when they join a gang—sometimes as young as eight. In fact, the gang problem in America is often referred to specifically as a youth problem because most gang members are in their teens and early 20s. However, members may be older in cities such as Los Angeles and Chicago, where certain gangs have been well-established for years. The latest statistics available from the National Gang Center indicate that about 35 percent of all gang members are under the age of 18.

Gang researchers believe that feeling distanced from one's own family may spur young people to seek out gangs. "The most frequently cited reason for people joining gangs is to belong,"[17] wrote criminal justice expert Kären M. Hess. A supportive and loving family with strong adult role models is a human necessity. Unfortunately, family upheaval is common in America. In some families, the home environment is hostile, or dangerous, due to child abuse, substance abuse by the parents or guardians, or family members who dislike each other. In some cases, the parents or older siblings are already in a gang, which makes joining the same gang seem like a natural decision for the younger children. Other families consist of only one parent, who must work long hours to provide for the family, meaning they are not often at home. This can be a problem if no substitute adult supervision is found; for example, in some families, the grandparents or an adult friend of the family watches the children and provides the socialization and supervision they need. If the children are left on their own, however, they are more likely to get into trouble.

Stress and conflict at home sometimes drive teens to join a gang so they feel like they have somewhere to escape to.

The most common image of a gang member is one from a family where at least one of the parents—generally, the father—is absent much or all of the time. This is frequently called a "broken home" because the nuclear family, which is made up of the parents and children, is not together. However, after completing a 10-year study of multiple gangs in multiple cities, researcher Martin Sanchez-Jankowski wrote in 1991, "I found that there were as many gang members from homes where the nuclear family was intact as there were from families where the father was absent."[18] There are many single parents who take good care of their children and provide a loving home, just as there are many two-parent families that do not. The biggest family-oriented risk factor for joining a gang is not the absence of a parent, but a lack of parental involvement and unconditional love at home. Those who receive little attention or support at home might envy what they see as a brotherhood or sisterhood in the gang lifestyle.

A SENSE OF BELONGING

"Gangs take root in schools for many reasons, but the primary attraction of gangs is their ability to respond to student needs that are not otherwise being met; they often provide youth with a sense of family and acceptance otherwise lacking in their lives."

–Gary Burnett and Garry Walz, social researchers

Gary Burnett and Garry Walz, "Gangs in the Schools," *ERIC Digest*, no. 99, July 1994. files.eric.ed.gov/fulltext/ED372175.pdf.

Another reason young people join gangs is because they believe gang life is exciting and glamorous. Stanley "Tookie" Williams, who cofounded the Los Angeles Crips gang in the 1970s and was executed by the state in 2005 for gang-related crimes, wrote, "I just found the streets to be more interesting than being at home … It felt liberating to be able to face the street adventures and to make my own decisions about what I should do."[19] The glorification of gangs in music and movies can give young adults the impression that joining a gang will make them rich, powerful, and respected. They may also be looking for protection from other gangs. In some cases, people ask to join one of the gangs in their neighborhood, but in many other cases, they are recruited in middle or high school by gang members "offering quick cash, guns, cars, girls, money, muscle; essentially, a (false) sense of empowerment,"[20] wrote former gang member Bill Lee. In reality, most find out after they join that the lifestyle is not what they were promised. Lee, who joined an Asian gang when he was eight years old, wrote,

> Many guys were bullied and turned to gangs for protection and revenge. We helped them settle scores, but they soon realized that bullying occurred within the gang as well, often more brutal. By then, it was too late to get out …
>
> When fellow gang members were attacked and killed, retaliation was not only justified—it was expected. And when your buddies

are jumping *someone, there was immense peer pressure to join in, whether you wanted to or not. There was also constant pressure to prove how tough you were.*[21]

Gangs may lie to potential members, telling them they are not actually a gang, just a group of people who hang out together, protect each other, and make money. They may take the recruit to parties and downplay the illegal activities the gang uses to make money, and they tend to target people who are complaining about their families, convincing them that they are correct to believe they are unloved and unwanted by everyone except the gang. Another tactic sometimes used is to do a favor for someone and then demand they join the gang as repayment.

The gang's symbols, such as special colors, hand signs, graffiti, and tattoos, are also attractive to many people. Historically, people have enjoyed the signs that they belong to an organization, whether it is a secretive organization such as a gang or an organization that is entirely innocent. For example, many people in the military enjoy wearing a uniform because it shows that they belong to that group.

Some gangs are so large that not all of the members know each other. Gang signs are hand symbols used to identify members. Sometimes innocent hand symbols such as this one are mistakn for gang signs.

Sometimes gangs do not need to be subtle at all when re-cruiting new members. Hannah Dreier, a journalist who spent a year reporting on MS-13—which is especially active in Long Island, a part of New York City—wrote, "Long Island teenagers tell me that when they show up to school, gang members sit down next to them at lunch and ask them to join. Many—worn down by loneliness, boredom and the threat of violence if they try to refuse—accept the invitation."[22]

Many gangs are selective about who they recruit, since a gang that grows too large is harder to control. Gangs recruit new members to replace members who have left or been killed as well as to gain access to resources a target may have, such as money. According to law enforcement agents in British Columbia, Canada, one of the reasons why gangs prefer to target young people is because they are less likely to have a criminal record. This means that if they are caught by police while doing some-thing for the gang, such as delivering drugs, they may receive a lighter sentence and possibly no time in jail. In contrast, people who have been in the gang for longer likely already have a crimi-nal history and would receive harsher punishments if caught.

Gangs and Gender

According to available statistics, most gang members are men; police gang experts believe that only about 7 percent of them are female, although—as with white gang members—many researchers think these estimates may be too low. "[Girls'] par-ticipation in gangs is more widespread than has typically been believed,"[23] wrote criminology professor Jody Miller. As with Native American gangs, the low numbers create a lack of inter-est in the study of female gang members, which contributes to a lack of data. The National Gang Center noted, "Nearly half of the gangs outside of the larger cities are reported to have female gang members, compared with approximately one in four in the larger cities. Of course, these results must be in-terpreted cautiously because of the sizable amount of missing data."[24] Some experts say female gang membership is increasing, but others believe people are simply paying more attention to them. Studies done by agencies that are not connected to law enforcement have found that female gang membership may be as high as 49 percent.

Prison Gangs

City streets are home to a large number of gangs in the United States, but a growing portion of the gang population exists in the prison system. Not all belonged to street gangs before their convictions, but those who join gangs in prison often have an impact on street gangs when they are released. According to the *Economist*, prison gangs did not exist until the 1950s, when the prison population had grown larger and more dangerous than it had been in the past. People began joining gangs for protection: They knew they were less likely to be harmed by other inmates if people were aware that the other members of the gang would punish the attacker. Many prison gangs are divided along racial lines because it is one of the easiest ways for members who might not have met before to identify each other. The other way is to get a tattoo of something the gang uses as a symbol. Prisoners can give each other tattoos by making their own tattoo gun and ink out of items they can access at the prison, but this is against prison rules, so they hide them from the guards.

Like street gangs, many prison gangs traffic drugs to make money. The *Economist* described why this is easier for people than dealing drugs alone:

> *Fail to pay a prison gang for your drugs and they have many more members who can kill you. Murder a dealer instead of paying him and his fellow gangsters will retaliate. Gangs can steal customers from individual dealers without worrying about revenge. And members can help facilitate trade [make it easier] from the outside after their release.*[1]

1. J. D., "Why Prisoners Join Gangs," *Economist*, November 12, 2014. www.economist.com/the-economist-explains/2014/11/12/why-prisoners-join-gangs.

Some major gangs in the United States today do not allow women to become members at all, although they may let women associate with them as girlfriends or helpers of male gang members. Some gangs include women not as true members but as employees, such as in drug and sex trafficking rings. A few gangs are true mixed-gender groups that allow women to become full-fledged members with the same gang privileges and responsibilities that male members have. Even fewer are all-female gangs.

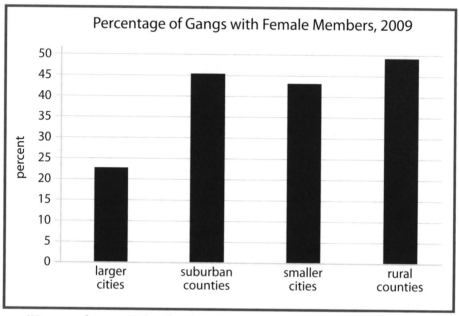

Women are far more likely to be allowed into a gang in the country than in a big city, as this information from the National Gang Center shows.

Across gang culture, girls and women are rarely given the same respect in the gang that male members receive from each other. Female gang members often assist the males, taking orders and willingly participating in criminal—and sometimes violent—activities but rarely having a say in what the gang plans or does. According to Hess, female gangsters "are often drug dependent and physically abused,"[25] which gives the male members control over them. In contrast, women in all-female gangs reported feeling safer and having fewer conflicts with each other.

In 2017, the Global Initiative Against Transnational Organized Crime published a study titled "Gangs, Violence, and the Role of Women and Girls" by Mark Shaw and Luke

In It for Life?

It is commonly stated that joining a gang is a lifelong commitment, and sometimes this is true. Leaving a gang is sometimes seen by the other members as a betrayal, leading to the threat of violence against the former member or their loved ones. This is especially true for high-ranking gang members, who are more likely to know the names of the other leaders and the details of all of the gang's criminal activities.

Leaving a gang sometimes requires actions as extreme as moving to a different city. For low-ranking members, however, getting out is often easier than expected. "The age distribution of gang members and virtually every study of gangs belies this conventional wisdom"[1] that gang membership is really for life, wrote Klein and Maxson. In fact, the National Gang Center reported that many people are only in a gang for one to two years. If they do not have strong ties to their fellow gang members, they may be able to simply stop attending gang activities, stop wearing their gang's colors or symbols, and change their phone number to make it harder for the gang to reach them. Between 40 and 60 percent of former gang members report drifting away like this, despite stories kept alive by current and former members that in order to be allowed to leave, someone must endure or commit violence. Experts recommend that people do not inform the gang that they intend to leave to minimize the threat of violence. Additionally, rival gangs who do not know the person has left the gang life may still target the former member or their loved ones, adding to the safety concerns.

Finding help and support outside the gang is an important part of leaving. Joining a club at school, joining a religious youth group, or getting a legitimate job are all ways people can ease their transition out of a gang. According to Christian Bolden, a researcher who has worked directly with gangs, "The young people I spoke to pointed to life events such as the death of a family member or close friend due to gang violence, joining the military, getting sentenced to prison or simply maturing out [as reasons for leaving]. The members I interviewed all knew of people who had left gangs without violence or retribution."[2] However, caution is still recommended in certain circumstances.

1. Malcolm W. Klein and Cheryl L. Maxson, *Street Gang Patterns and Policies.* New York, NY: Oxford University Press, 2006, p. 153.

2. Christian Bolden, "Everything You Think You Know About Gangs Is Wrong," Talking Points Memo, December 26, 2013. talkingpointsmemo.com/cafe/everything-you-think-you-know-about-gangs-is-wrong.

Lee Skywalker. The two researchers interviewed more than 30 adult female gang members in Cape Town, South Africa, where gang activity is high. They noted that "not all interviews yield the same amount or quality of data,"[26] but despite this problem, several trends were common in most of the interviewees' stories. These included the following:

- Like men, women and girls tend to look to gangs for the love and connection they do not receive from their families. They also look for protection; according to what the women told the researchers, "in places where gangs hold so much sway and violent power and capacity, not joining a gang 'makes you far more vulnerable, than joining one.'"[27]

- Most of the interviewed women described rape and sexual abuse directed toward them from fellow gang members. Sadly, this is also something most of them experienced from family members even before joining a gang. The researchers noted that the "young women were often attracted to the same violent, abusive and unreliable men that had shaped their own child- and young adulthoods."[28] If they try to report this abuse to police, sometimes they are dismissed; other times, unfortunately, they are further abused by the police. In some cases, male gang members offer police officers a female gang member as a bribe, to encourage the officer not to arrest the other gang members. The researchers noted, "Female gang members therefore are seen as available, marginalised (thus unlikely to be believed) and therefore easy to abuse, with few consequences for the officials involved."[29]

- Female gang members tend to be monitored closely and controlled by male gang members, limiting their freedom and making it harder for them to leave the gang. Most of the interviewees described being marked with tattoos or scars when they had consumed too much alcohol or too many drugs to consent. These marks later made it hard for them to get legitimate jobs.

In many gangs, the female members are abused by the male members, both physically and sexually. Some become pregnant. Shown here is a Colombian woman who used to be a gang member with her daughter.

It is clear that there are many reasons why someone might want to join a gang, and people often do not know the realities of gang life before they commit. The lures of friendship, power, respect, and especially money are difficult to resist in certain circumstances. Gangs frequently form as moneymaking operations, so they can be a type of business—one that often relies on violence to keep it running.

THE CHANGING GANG CULTURE

"Gang membership is not what it used to be. Members I interviewed were not sure exactly who was in their own gang or how many people were members ... they were mainly focused on their own close-knit subgroup of four or five people. Switching from [one] gang to another, or quitting 'the life,' unthinkable betrayals in movies, are common today."

–Christian Bolden, professor of criminal justice at Loyola University in New Orleans, Louisiana

Christian Bolden, "Everything You Think You Know About Gangs Is Wrong," Talking Points Memo, December 26, 2013. talkingpointsmemo.com/cafe/everything-you-think-you-know-about-gangs-is-wrong.

CHAPTER 3

The Gang Lifestyle

Regardless of the ethnicity, immigrant status, age, or gender of their members, gangs almost always form in impoverished areas—places where living conditions are unpleasant and where good jobs and a good education seem out of reach. A sense of hopelessness and pointlessness, of having been forgotten or purposely ignored by the rest of America, is overwhelming in such places. Young men, in particular, crave the chance to be successful, have good-paying jobs, support themselves and their families, and be respected figures in their communities. Gangs falsely promise to help them meet all those goals.

Living in poverty is considered the single strongest driving force behind the formation of gangs in America and is also the most significant factor that gangs throughout American history have had in common. The harsh realities of life in a desperately poor neighborhood often remain constant over time, and crime may be the only type of employment that many gang members think is available to them. "Sadly, education does not provide the same financial rewards for lower-income youth as it does for youth in middle-income groups,"[30] wrote social development researchers Ian Bannon and Maria C. Correia. Even if someone graduates from high school or college, they may have difficulty finding a job. This can be due to multiple factors, such as their race or gender, a lack of good jobs close enough to get to every day, or a lack of connections to potential employers.

Gangs are more than just social clubs of people who live in the same neighborhood and share the same background.

The definition of a gang, according to the U.S. Department of Justice, is a group whose activities include crime, and most types of crimes that gangs commit are done for profit, either to make money for the gang directly or to protect its moneymaking methods. "[Gang members] believe the profits from crime are worth the risk of punishment," wrote Larry Siegel. "It may be their only significant chance for gain and profit."[31]

Poverty, Gangs, and Violence

In many countries, there is a stigma, or negative view, around being poor. For example, many people in the United States equate economic status with morality—they believe people are either rich or poor because they deserve to be. The rich are viewed as hardworking and determined, while the poor are seen as lazy and wasteful. In one 2001 study,

> researchers from Kansas State and Rice Universities asked subjects to rate how well a variety of words described different social groups. Compared to their ratings of middle-class people, and given no information except economic status, the average subject described poor people as 39 percent more "unpleasant," 95 percent more "unmotivated," and twice as "dirty."[32]

These types of associations—which are generally false and disproportionately affect black, Latinx, and Native American groups—tend to make people who live in poverty feel angry. The desire to be respected instead of looked down on can be a strong motivating factor for joining a gang. According to the website How Stuff Works, "The notion of respect drives gang life almost completely, and for many gang members, gaining respect means committing violent crimes."[33] Anyone who does something a gang member sees as disrespectful—whether it is a stranger insulting them or a member of a rival gang trying to sell drugs on another gang's turf—is likely to find themselves targeted for violence.

Violence is the most pressing issue that gangs create. Gang members tend to be territorial and fiercely loyal to their own gang. At the same time, gangs view each other as rivals competing for the same area of a neighborhood, the same share of income, or the same power and influence in their community. Gangs frequently challenge one another, and those challenges can be dangerously violent. Most gang members see it as their duty to defend the gang against rivals, and they do so with no regard for the innocent people who happen to be in the area at the time.

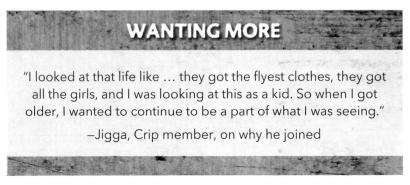

WANTING MORE

"I looked at that life like ... they got the flyest clothes, they got all the girls, and I was looking at this as a kid. So when I got older, I wanted to continue to be a part of what I was seeing."

–Jigga, Crip member, on why he joined

"Kendrick Lamar–Reebok Ventilators," YouTube video, 2.17, posted by Top Dawg Entertainment, July 18, 2015. www.youtube.com/watch?time_continue=63&v=_T2XcE9UhWl.

Innocent people often get caught in the crossfire of gang warfare.

Drive-by shootings are one of the most feared forms of gang violence because it is common for innocent people to be hurt. According to the Los Angeles Police Department (LAPD), "Members from one gang will seek out the homes, vehicles or hang-outs of a rival gang and, using an assortment of weapons, will drive by and shoot at members of that gang. Usually, the gang member will yell out the gang name or a slogan so the attacked gang will know who was responsible."[34] Since the attacking gang is identified, the attacked gang knows who to retaliate

An Infamous Feud

Two of the best-known, longest-running gangs in the United States are the Bloods and the Crips. Both gangs have existed for more than 45 years, but few people know much about them aside from what they see in fictional media.

The Crips, founded in 1969 in Los Angeles, is one of the largest gangs in the world. Some smaller gangs are actually sub-gangs of the Crips, called "sets." In the 1980s, the gang made a huge amount of money by selling cocaine, and by 2000, about 600 sets existed. Famous rappers such as Snoop Dogg, Coolio, and Xzibit have been in the Crips at one time or another. The identifying color of the Crips is blue, and people who are not in a gang are warned to avoid wearing anything of this color in certain areas where the gang has a heavy presence. People are also warned to avoid wearing red in case they are mistaken for a member of the Crips' rival gang, the Bloods. This gang, founded in 1972 to provide members with protection against the Crips, has become another of the largest gangs in the world, expanding throughout the United States and some parts of Canada. Like the Crips, they have sets in multiple cities. In addition to rapper Cardi B, some famous Bloods have included Gucci Mane and Waka Flocka Flame.

The Crips have adopted blue as their signature color, while the Bloods wear red. However, they do not necessarily wear these colors all the time, as this photo of several Crips members shows.

against, leading to a continuation of the cycle of violence. Gangs also sometimes perform drive-by mass shootings simply to inspire fear of the gang in the surrounding community. This is because in their view, fear leads to respect.

What Do Gangs Do?

Gang researchers and police note that it is difficult, if not impossible, to accurately document gang violence. As the LAPD explained, "many gang activities are frequently shared by a large portion of society."[35] In other words, while a gang may sell drugs or rob a store, so do people who are not in gangs. Also, in almost any gang in America, the number one rule is that gang "brothers" do not snitch on one another: Come what may, a gang member will never give police information that could send another gang member to prison, even if the person who was caught must go to prison in their friend's place. Though the gangs of America are widely diverse, these two demands—self-sacrifice and the expectation of lifelong loyalty—are common to almost all of them. Those who follow this code make it difficult for police to accurately follow gang activity.

The believability of a gang as a tight and unbreakable group does not always hold up when the gang is under pressure, however. When their gang activity gets them in trouble with the law, many gang members are quick to break the no-snitching rule the gang expects them to uphold. "They'll tell you morning, noon, and night that 'these are my brothers, these are my associates, and we're in this blood in and blood out' kind of thing," said Tim Twining, chief deputy district attorney in Denver, Colorado. The reality, he said, is that snitching is common. "When the chips really fall on the table, and it's 'you're going to prison for the rest of your life or you tell the truth,' we'll often get the truth."[36]

Even so, according to the National Gang Center, "most law enforcement agencies neither regularly nor reliably record local offenses as 'gang-related' … The sole exception to this practice pertains to homicides [murder], where most agencies report tracking the number of gang-related homicides. Thus, at a national level, this is currently the only offense for which data are available."[37]

Committing acts of vandalism, such as breaking windows or painting graffiti on walls, is one crime many gangs are known to commit.

It is believed to be common practice in many cities for gang members to rob stores, steal cars, vandalize property, or mug strangers to take their cash and other valuables. Small, localized street gangs may limit their activities to these types of crimes. According to How Stuff Works, "Daily gang life is generally not very exciting. Gang members sleep late, sit around the neighborhood, drink and do drugs and possibly go to a meeting place in the evening … They may work a street corner selling drugs or commit petty crimes like vandalism or theft."[38] Many gangs also demand protection money from business owners, street vendors, and even taxi drivers who operate in the gang's neighborhood. Those who do not pay may get bullied and harassed, their businesses may be vandalized, and their customers may be chased away by the gang.

Larger, more organized gangs may also run crime rings, or associations that collectively commit a type of crime to make a profit. One such gang is Tango Blast, the largest gang in Houston, Texas. The Texas Department of Public Safety (DPS) has reported that it is aware Tango Blast is involved in human smuggling (helping people cross international borders illegally) and human trafficking (transporting people—generally women and children—across borders for the purpose of exploiting them sexually or forcing them into labor). However, even when law enforcement is aware of a gang's illegal activities, it is frequently difficult for them to catch the gang in the act or gather enough evidence to prosecute them in court. Additionally, not all smugglers who are caught are connected to a gang. According to the

Washington Post, "Smugglers are often just low-level independent operators, loosely connected to others, trying to make a buck … 'To get migrants through segments of the border you do not need organized crime,' [author and human smuggling researcher Gabriella] Sanchez said. 'You need an immigration agent [to bribe].'"[39]

It seems to be common knowledge that most gangs are also heavily involved in the drug trade, but according to researcher James C. Howell, "youth gang drug trafficking is characterized mainly by public perception rather than by scientific knowledge."[40] Few, if any, studies have been performed on this issue since the 1990s. While some gangs are known to sell drugs, others are not, and Howell pointed out that "typical street gang structures are inadequate to organize and manage drug trafficking operations."[41]

HOW GANGS TAKE CONTROL

"Everyone must pay us … if the taxis wanna … drive through our area then they must pay to do so … Even if we kill someone we can tol (reverse) that case. The case file or court docket will just go missing. It is easy to get to people if you have money."

–"Grace Jones," Cape Town gang member

Quoted in Mark Shaw and Luke Lee Skywalker, "Gangs, Violence and the Role of Women and Girls: Emerging Themes and Policy and Programme Options Drawn from Interviews with Female Gang Members in Cape Town," The Global Initiative Against Transnational Organized Crime, March 2017, p. 20. www.unodc.org/res/cld/bibliography/gangs-violence-and-the-role-of-women-and-girls_-emerging-themes-and-policy-programme-options-drawn-from-interviews-with-female-gang-members-in-cape-town_html/tgiatoc-women-in-gangs-policy-note-1837-lo-res1.pdf.

Organization and Expansion

Many people assumed in the past that gangs spread out across the country so they could expand their drug trafficking operations, but a 1996 study found that this was only true in about one-third of cities that saw an expansion of gang activity. In most cases, gang members moved for reasons such as a desire to be closer to friends and family, and very few of them recruited others to the gang after they had moved. Thus, contrary to concerns that the gang problem is growing because existing gangs are concentrating on expanding, it is likely that when gangs appear for the first time in a new community, they are formed on the spot instead of moving in from a different city.

Prohibition-era gangs gave rise to modern gangs that still operate with the goal of conducting business to make money. Many gang experts, however, believe that today's gangs are not nearly as businesslike as their 1920s predecessors. Some do still have an identifiable hierarchy, or structure, with the leaders at the top and the new recruits at the bottom. In the world of organized crime, the leaders plan what happens and give orders to their recruits, similar to the military. In this type of gang, these recruits are the ones most often in the line of fire from other gangs and the ones most likely to get caught for the gang's crimes. Meanwhile, those who organize the gang's crimes often remain untouched, and the gang continuously recruits new members to replace the ones who are lost. Despite the arrests of many of its members, a gang whose leaders are well protected from prosecution may continue to thrive and grow. One of the best examples of this is the late 1930s gang boss Al Capone. Police knew Capone had ordered murders and other crimes to be carried out, but he was so well protected that when he was finally arrested, it was for income tax evasion—the only thing police could actually prove he had

The traditional image of a gangster is someone similar to Al Capone (shown here): a well-dressed, older man who is part of an organized crime ring such as the Mafia. However, most gang members do not look like this, and most gangs are not organized enough to commit many major crimes.

done. Organized crime rings are structured so that "only the leader knows every precise movement of all the gang members, which makes the job of law enforcement difficult," wrote retired police detective and gang expert Edward Burns. "A gang's methods of operation are designed to resist a knockout blow"[42] such as the arrest of multiple lower-level gang members by law enforcement. Organized crime rings are also better at hiding their activities, so they are less likely to be prosecuted than disorganized street gangs.

DODGING THE POLICE

"Well, drug sales could be made in cars, in houses, on the streets ... They happen everywhere. I don't know if there's a center or central place where they happen ... The police bust some people here, it goes somewhere else. It just moves around."

—Maurice, gang member

Quoted in Michael K. Carlie, "The Gang Culture," Into the Abyss: A Personal Journey into the World of Street Gangs, 2002. people.missouristate.edu/MichaelCarlie/what_I_learned_about/gangs/crimes_gangs_commit.htm

However, the majority of gangs are really quite disorganized, said Chris Mathers, who has worked with gangs as an undercover officer for the Federal Bureau of Investigation (FBI) and the Drug Enforcement Administration (DEA). Many experts believe that gangs are still simply groups of people clinging to the edges of mainstream society and making a desperate attempt to earn a living in an environment where few other kinds of jobs and financial prospects exist. "Most gangs couldn't put a pound of grass [marijuana] together if you relied on the gang as an entity to do so,"[43] he wrote.

The idea that all American gangs are sophisticated crime organizations may overestimate their criminal capability. Most gang researchers believe few U.S. gangs have enough organization or control over their members to actually operate the kind of drug cartels (criminal organizations that specialize in drug trafficking) that exist in Mexico and South America, but

Most street gangs are not part of organized crime rings. They tend to spend their time committing petty (less serious) crimes and fighting with rival gangs to defend their turf.

some U.S. gangs do have a partnership with drug cartels. The cartels supply the drugs, while multiple U.S.-based gangs help move drugs across the national border and into American cities. "One gang, before being stopped by federal authorities, had a cocaine distribution network that stretched across five states,"[44] wrote youth violence researcher Elizabeth Kandel Englander. Getting control over such a spread-out gang requires cooperation and communication among many different local, state, and national police forces, often making it a long and difficult process to address gang crime.

Some people believe the gang problem is growing, but experts say that is a difficult thing to measure. In an interview with *U.S. News & World Report* in 2015, James C. Howell stated that the number of gangs and gang members had increased in the previous five years. He noted that this was likely due to larger gangs breaking apart and forming more, smaller gangs. This is not a new phenomenon, however. Any large gang, regardless of the way it is organized, runs the risk of getting too big to be governed tightly by its leaders. In fact, the more structure a gang has, the less happy its members often are within it. Some gang members want more money and power and may dislike being told what to do by the leaders of their gang. When this happens, new gangs tend to splinter off from the original ones to make different gangs, and formerly lower-ranked members then have a chance to become leaders in the new gang. In a 10-year study of major gangs in New York City, Boston, and Los Angeles in

Gangs in Sweden

For years, Sweden has consistently been ranked one of the best countries to live in. Compared to other countries, it has better than average "environmental quality, civic engagement, education and skills, work-life balance, health status, subjective well-being, income and wealth, jobs and earnings, housing, personal safety, and social connections."[1] However, even Sweden has to deal with gangs. In the city of Stockholm, violence has been on the rise since 2011, mainly because of "street gangs running small-time drug operations in big cities."[2] These gangs, which are not well organized, defend their turf with illegal weapons, and the *Economist* reported in 2018 that some gangs have even attacked police with hand grenades.

Because of the high quality of life and stable economy in Sweden, experts are unsure of why gangs are more common there today. The most likely explanation, according to researchers, is that Sweden takes good care of its natural-born citizens but fails to help immigrants access good education and good jobs. With few choices left, frustrated young immigrant men form gangs and turn to crime to help them make money. To address this problem, "the government has provided additional funding for integrating migrants, imposed harsher punishments for gun crimes and granted a weapons amnesty."[3] A weapons amnesty is a policy intended to get weapons off the street; people can turn in the illegal weapons they already have without fear of punishment. This is a better alternative to many than being caught and arrested while using an illegal weapon. Experts hope these measures will decrease Swedish gang activity.

1. "Sweden," OECD Better Life Index, accessed on August 10, 2018. www.oecdbetterlifeindex.org/countries/sweden/

2. "Why Are Young Men in Sweden Shooting Each Other?," *Economist*, March 8, 2018. www.economist.com/europe/2018/03/08/why-are-young-men-in-sweden-shooting-each-other.

3. "Why Are Young Men in Sweden Shooting Each Other?," *Economist*.

the 1980s, Martin Sanchez-Jankowski found that when a gang collapsed, "it was either incorporated into the structure of a rival gang (much like a takeover in the business world) or broke into factions that reorganized into a new gang or gangs."[45] Some gangs' populations have not changed much over time; for example, MS-13 has had about 10,000 members in the United States for more than 10 years, showing that new members join at about the same rate that old members leave—either voluntarily or by getting arrested or killed. However, many gangs are known to promote themselves and actively try to recruit new members, so it is likely that at least a few gangs are expanding.

CHAPTER 4

Promoting and Recruiting

The attraction of gang life must be overwhelmingly strong for potential members, because getting into a gang is generally neither painless nor easy. Members must go to great lengths to prove themselves worthy. Most gangs require potential members to take part in some kind of initiation before they can join. One of the most common is a jump-in—a ritual in which the recruit must fight a group of several gang members for a certain amount of time. Those who do not surrender or back down during this fierce beating earn the gang's acceptance. Those who fail to impress the gang at a jump-in, on the other hand, are excluded from membership, and some gangs have been known to kill recruits who show weakness during a jump-in. Other initiations include performing a drive-by shooting against a gang's rival, being "punched in" (hit very hard on the chest, right over the heart—a ritual that has killed some recruits), and being "sexed in" (requiring female members to perform sexual acts on one or more of the male gang members). However, since the early 2000s, this has been changing. Gang researcher Christian Bolden reported in 2013 that many gangs now allow new members to be "blessed in," or approved by current members, without having to perform a dangerous initiation. This is a problem, he said, because it may encourage even more people to join gangs.

Movies, Television, and Video Games

Part of the reason why a gang's promises of wealth, power, and respect sound believable is the portrayal of gang life in the

Scary Myths

Gangs are often blamed for any poorly-understood act of violence, even when the individual committing the crime was not part of any gang. The rise of email and social media has made it even easier to spread rumors, resulting in an increase in fear—often unnecessarily. Most of these emails and posts center around the idea that a random victim has been chosen to be killed as a way for a new gang member to be initiated, although none are based in fact. They include stories of gang members flashing their car headlights at a random car to indicate to the new recruit which driver has been marked as the victim; gang members hiding in the backseat of a car while the driver is filling up at the gas station, then killing them after they pull away from the pump; and gang members using various tactics to get drivers to stop and get out of their cars so they could be shot.

According to Snopes, a website that investigates and debunks urban legends, "There have been instances of initiations into street gangs that led to the murder of random victims, but they are rare. Generally, they don't involve gang hopefuls being clearly commanded by their overlords to take the lives of the haphazardly-selected."[1] Instead, the website noted, these random killings generally happen by accident while the initiates are committing a different type of crime, such as robbery. Most gang initiations involve violence directed at the new gang member, not an outsider, and the same techniques have been used for years. Emails or internet posts that describe a "new type of gang initiation" sweeping an area should be viewed with distrust and researched by the reader.

1. Barbara Mikkelson, "Gang Initiation by Chase Down," Snopes, July 12, 2011. www.snopes.com/fact-check/deadly-chase-down/.

media. It has been glorified for decades, and this has shaped not only the way the non-gang population thinks of gangs, but also the way gang members think of themselves. According to author and professor James Finckenauer, this started with organized crime rings during Prohibition. Because this anti-alcohol

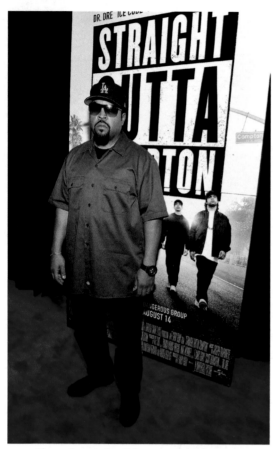

Shown here is Ice Cube, one of the founding members of N.W.A., which is the rap group at the center of Straight Outta Compton.

policy "was hugely unpopular, the men who stood up to it were heralded [praised] as heroes, not criminals. 'It was the start of their image as people who can thumb their noses at bad laws and at the establishment,' Finckenauer said."[46] Similarly, some people see street gangs as groups of people who do whatever they want, whether or not there are laws against it. This makes gangs attractive to people who dislike law enforcement officials.

Television, film, and video games are partly responsible for creating the idea that gang life is exciting and even desirable. For example, in 1972, the movie *The Godfather*, about the Mafia lifestyle, was released and later won three Oscars. *The Godfather* and its two sequels became one of the most famous and popular movie trilogies of all time. Since *The Godfather*, movies about gangs have been numerous and popular. Among them are 1991's *Boyz 'n the Hood*, which was about inner-city gang life in Los Angeles and was later nominated for two Oscars; *Gangs of New York*, a movie about gang life in the 1800s, which earned 10 Oscar nominations in 2003; 2007's *American Gangster*, which received two Oscar nominations; and *Straight Outta Compton*, which received one Oscar nomination in 2016. Some people suggested that *Straight Outta Compton*, which was praised by many critics and audiences, did not receive more nominations because it focused mainly on black Americans.

Behind the Scenes of
Straight Outta Compton

Straight Outta Compton tells the story of rap group N.W.A's rise to fame in the late 1980s. Only two of the group's members were in an actual street gang, but their music celebrated gang culture, and the group did get involved in gang fights. According to an article in *L.A. Weekly*, Dr. Dre—one of the group's members—"joined forces with the Piru Bloods-affiliated Suge Knight to form Death Row Records ... Knight and his associates used force to get what they wanted, and Dre eventually tired of his collaborators being ... intimidated or even beaten."[1] Because of this early association with the Bloods, the filmmakers were not allowed into Crips territory years later, even though it was where Dre and several of the other group members had grown up. In fact, the producers had to hire someone to negotiate with gangs so the filmmakers could walk safely on certain streets. *L.A. Weekly* stated, "Unwittingly, the film reignited old vendettas [grudges], renewed simmering gangland tensions and even led to one man's death"[2] when one of Knight's longtime rivals was hired by the film company. At least one drive-by shooting also took place near a filming location, although it was never made clear whether it was gang-associated. Even though nearly 30 years separated the movie's production and the group's gang involvement, violence was still a problem because of how fiercely the Bloods and Crips defend their turf. This shows how hard it is to break the cycle of gang violence.

1. Ben Westhoff, "Filming *Straight Outta Compton* Got a Lot More Real than Anyone Intended," *L.A. Weekly*, August 11, 2015. www.laweekly.com/music/filming-straight-outta-compton-got-a-lot-more-real-than-anyone-intended-5893236.
2. Westhoff, "Filming Straight Outta Compton."

Even TV has had a gang presence, as in the award-winning, Mafia-themed drama series *The Sopranos*. However, not all gang-themed TV shows glorify that life. In the show *The Wire*, which ran from 2002 to 2008 and has often been called one of the best shows in television history, gang members were major characters, but the show's overall message was about how society has contributed to the problem. According to Alan Sepinwall, author of *The Revolution Was Televised*, "There were always cops, and always criminals, but the series used them to make various points about the rotting state of the American city—and, by extension, the broken condition of America itself … the world of *The Wire* is one where almost no one is willing to work in a non-traditional way, and the few that do tend to get punished for it."[47] When no one changes their behavior, the series shows, things inevitably stay the way they have always been, and no progress can be made.

THE EFFECTS OF VIOLENT GAMES

"So, less empathy, pleasure in the pain of others, well practiced criminal behavior, decreased capacity for mature decision making. These are just a few of the potential side effects of violent videogame play."

—Dr. Darcia F. Narvaez, psychology professor

Darcia F. Narvaez, "Playing Violent Video Games: Good or Bad?," *Psychology Today*, November 9, 2010. www.psychologytoday.com/us/blog/moral-landscapes/201011/playing-violent-video-games-good-or-bad.

The popularity of the gang theme in American TV and movies is evidence that Americans are enthralled with the gang lifestyle on screen. Some video games take this a step further by allowing players to put themselves in a gangster's shoes. For example, in *Grand Theft Auto: San Andreas*, players report being able to provoke gang wars by shooting three members of an opposing gang. Winning the gang war allows them to take over certain territories, which helps them eventually win the game by acquiring more money and more respect for the gang. Since video games are produced for entertainment, this install-ment of *Grand Theft Auto* may make young adults see gang life as fun and exciting. Additionally, since they can stop and put away the game at any time and their actions have no effect on

The Grand Theft Auto *games have been highly controversial due to all the violence the gameplay requires.*

the real world, the game may minimize how damaging gang activity can be.

There have been a number of studies on children's exposure to violent games. Some have shown children to be more aggressive after exposure to violence in media, but other studies have not shown this. There is no conclusive link between violent media and violent behavior, but some studies point to an increase in aggression by children exposed to violence, especially if they do not have strong social connections and if they learn to associate violence with reward—for example, the way *Grand Theft Auto* requires violent actions for someone to win the game.

Gangsta Rap

Hip-hop music, which originated in the 1970s, quickly rocketed to chart-topping status, and the rap and hip-hop genre is one of the most popular kinds of music in America today. In the 1980s and 1990s, some hip-hop stars branched into a new music genre called gangsta rap, which is still popular today. Many popular gangsta rap songs have titles and lyrics that make undeniable references to gangs, such as "Why We Thugs" by Ice Cube and "Gangsta's Paradise" by Coolio. Ice Cube and Coolio, like several other gangsta rap stars, were affiliated with gangs before their music became famous.

Gangsta rap, although very popular, is also controversial. People have protested the music for its bad language, violent lyrics, and promotion of brutality against police. Gangsta rap songs and music videos are also notorious for their sexist portrayals of women. The music has been harshly criticized for idolizing gangs and encouraging young people to take part in a lifestyle of crime, murder, and abuse of women. In fact, in 1990, the release of an album by gangsta rap group the Geto Boys was delayed; the record company the group was with at the time refused to distribute it due to its glorification of violence and explicit sexual lyrics. The late C. DeLores Tucker, former head of the National Political Congress of Black Women, was one outspoken critic of gangsta rap. "A gangster is a criminal," Tucker said, adding that "gangsta rap is criminal activity."[48]

Defenders of gangsta rap, meanwhile, claim that music alone does not force or even encourage anyone to join a gang or commit gang-related crimes and that the majority of this music's audience are not gang members at all. Many of the rappers themselves have argued that their songs are expressions of the frustration and pain they have experienced as a result of poverty and racism. "A record can't make nobody do anything," N.W.A's MC Ren told *Newsweek* in 1991. "Sometimes doing a record is just my way of getting back, 'cause when [police] got you jacked up on a car, and they got a gun to your head, you can't say [anything]. Doing records I can speak out. When people listen to the record, that's their way of speaking back."[49]

THE DANGER OF GANGSTA RAP

"When I shot people, the first thing I did was put on a [gangsta rap] record ... Rap music is the driving force of the destruction of a lot of people. I don't want it to be that for these kids."

—Derek Brown, former gang member and current youth mentor

Quoted in Dawn M. Turner, "Ex-Gang Member Talks About Rap Music's Influence," *Chicago Tribune*, November 5, 2015. www.chicagotribune.com/news/columnists/ct-rap-music-gang-influence-turner-20151105-column.html.

Nevertheless, many experts do believe that the widespread popularity of gangsta rap music helps explain why so many young people in America seem to be attracted to the gang lifestyle. Some rap songs imply that there is a link between listening to rap music and participating in gang life, such as Ice Cube's 2008 hit "Gangsta Rap Made Me Do It." In some communities where gang presence is either new or has recently been on the rise, police also say there is a definite connection between the appearance of hip-hop clubs that play gangsta rap and a rise in street violence. "When you have music that says it's basically O.K. to treat women poorly, to steal things and to confront and shoot police officers ... you'll attract a small percentage of the population that wants to lead the thug life,"[50] said Thomas Harris, a police lieutenant in Colorado Springs, Colorado.

One notable exception to gangsta rap as a promotion of gang life is rapper Kendrick Lamar. Lamar, who grew up in Compton, California, felt like gang culture was an unavoidable part of life for a long time. In an interview with *GRM Daily*, his interviewer said, "Obviously the gang culture history in L.A. is deep to the point where ... your gang affiliation might be specific to go back as far as your parents or your grandparents or, you know, like I said, something that's really deeply ingrained in the city."[51] Lamar agreed, noting that it felt strange to him to be in other cities and not have to consider which gangs someone he encountered might be associated with.

Because he grew up in this environment but has also traveled to other places—including South Africa, where he said he learned important things he was not taught growing up—Lamar has said that he wants to use his fame to end gang warfare in and around Los Angeles and unite the Bloods and Crips. In 2015, he said he deliberately avoided making catchy songs on his album *To Pimp a Butterfly* because he wanted people to really listen to and think about the lyrics—which he feels send important messages—instead of just hearing the beat.

There is little doubt that music and movies with gang themes glorify gangs and create an interest in the gang culture; however, gangs have been around for hundreds of years—much longer than radio, television, or movie theaters have existed in America. Modern-day media may help create ideas about gangs that capture people's imagination, but the real attraction to the gang lifestyle predates the media and probably exists much closer to the gang itself. A gang's success depends less on the media's glorification of it than on its own ability to convince potential members that it is desirable to belong to a gang.

Kendrick Lamar has been outspoken about his desire to end gang culture.

Gang Graffiti

The presence of graffiti is often the first sign of a gang's presence in a neighborhood. Gangs use graffiti to mark territory, honor fallen members, and challenge other gangs. Most gang graffiti is written simply, although some gangs will write their name in an elaborate style of large letters which are referred to as *placas*, an Old English style that has looped, pointed, and boxed or squared letters. Such graffiti may include the name of the gang and its individual members along with gang symbols or numbers identifying the gang. Gangs competing for the same turf often insult each other by writing over graffiti; for example, if a particular gang member's name is crossed out,

Kendrick Lamar's Reebok Ventilators

Aside from writing thoughtful lyrics and being outspoken against gang violence in interviews, another way Lamar is using his fame and newfound fortune to try to unite gangs is by creating a line of Reebok sneakers. The sneakers are white with the word "red" stitched on the heel on the right shoe and "blue" on the left, to represent the Bloods and Crips coming together. Inside, under the tongues of both shoes, is the word "neutral." In a video by Top Dawg Entertainment, a Blood called G. Weed and a Crip called Jigga sat down together to talk about the shoes and Lamar's overall influence on the Compton gang scene. Both agreed that their involvement in gangs started with things they saw and heard when they were children.

Regarding Lamar's music as well as the shoes, G. Weed said, "You got people like Kendrick that's, you know, promoting unity, you know what I mean? And everything start with kids. That make these kids wanna be cool with each other, no matter what neighborhood they grew up in."[1] Jigga agreed, saying that the message of the shoes "is just about a whole lot of peace and unity ... and Kendrick is just really giving us a reason and giving us an understanding of why we should have unity or why we should really wanna do this ... We taking steps together."[2] While neither shoes nor music alone will end gang violence, both are encouraging current gang members to put aside their differences and work together to achieve peace.

1. "Kendrick Lamar–Reebok Ventilators," YouTube video, 2:17, posted by Top Dawg Entertainment, July 18, 2015. www.youtube.com/watch?time_continue=63&v=_T2XcE9UhWI.
2. "Kendrick Lamar–Reebok Ventilators," YouTube video.

it often indicates that they have been marked to be killed by a rival gang.

According to the LAPD, gang graffiti is dangerous because it "is meant to create a sense of intimidation and may increase the sense of fear within a neighborhood ... When a neighborhood is marked with graffiti indicating territorial dominance, the entire area and its inhabitants become targets for violence."[52] This is something business owners and organization leaders in places with high gang activity need to consider. According to the Nonprofit Risk Management Center, which gives nonprofit leaders advice on how to reduce the risks associated with running an organization, "Allowing gang related graffiti to remain on your premises is an invitation for other gangs to cover it with theirs—possibly creating a gang war on your doorstep. Graffiti should be removed as soon as possible."[53]

A graffiti insult is a serious offense in the gang world and can set off a killing spree, but graffiti can also serve positive purposes: Police use it to track which gangs are claiming which territories and which gangs are rivals with each other. However, it is important to note that not all graffiti is gang-related. Most graffiti artists create works of art to show off their skill to each other and gain respect within the community, not to promote gang violence, and many have reported that gang members respect their work. For this reason, some communities have used graffiti to fight graffiti; for example, in 2009, officials in Chesterton, England, set aside space in their subway system and encouraged young artists to paint whatever they wanted—as long as it was artistic or positive—in an attempt to avoid having negative graffiti placed there.

Gang graffiti tends to have gang names or symbols in it, such as this graffiti in El Salvador (right). In contrast, graffiti that is not done by gangs is often more artistic (left).

Recruiting New Members

Earning notoriety (fame from bad deeds) and admiration within their own neighborhood or part of town is the main way most gangs expand. Despite movies and music that might portray the gang lifestyle as heroic or exciting to anyone who watches or listens, those who join gangs generally do so not just because they saw a movie or heard a song but because there is a gang in their neighborhood to join. Most advertising for gangs takes place on the street, by word of mouth. Young people who live in a gang's neighborhood are surrounded by constant advertisements of the gang lifestyle, and their nearness to actual gang members has a much stronger pull on potential members than gang movies or music do. Gang researchers Scott H. Decker and Barrik Van Winkle studied gangs in St. Louis, Missouri, in the early 1990s and discovered that "in every instance, joining the gang was the result of a process that evolved over a period of time … [Members] had grown up in the same neighborhood as other gang members and had done things with them for a lengthy period of time."[54] In some cases,

From the time they are born, children start learning from the adults around them. If the things they learn are negative, they are likely to copy those negative behaviors as they grow older.

family members such as parents or older siblings have already joined a gang, leading younger children to grow up believing that it is a normal way of life. This suggests that, while gang-related media may reinforce the image of gang membership as cool and desirable, actually growing up around gangs is a much more important factor behind most young people's interest in joining a gang. "It ain't just something you come and pick up," said a member of the North Side Mafia gang in Denver. "This is something that's put into you from when you're a little kid."[55]

LEARNING FROM FAMILY

"When you around five or six, your brain start sponging and absorbing things and you start hearing things and my older brothers were saying 'Blood,' you know what I mean? So I figured it out on my own."

–G. Weed, Blood member, on why he joined

"Kendrick Lamar—Reebok Ventilators," YouTube video, 2:17, posted by Top Dawg Entertainment, July 18, 2015. www.youtube.com/watch?time_continue=63&v=_T2XcE9UhWI.

Gangs on Social Media

As social media has become increasingly entwined in daily life, there is evidence that some gangs have begun to use it as well. In a survey of 137 teen gang members, 74 percent reported using the internet to promote the gang they belong to. According to researchers, it does not appear that they typically use the internet to recruit new members, but their posts have been shown to fuel violence between rival gangs. The National Gang Intelligence Center wrote in 2009, "Gang members often use cell phones and the Internet to communicate and promote their illicit activities" and to "boast about their gang membership and related activities."[56] A new term—cyber banging—has been coined to describe this type of action. This comes from the word gangbanging, which has been used for years to describe the violent criminal actions of gangs.

Many gangs have a presence on social networking websites such as Facebook and YouTube, so it is easier and faster for them to mock members of opposing gangs and watch videos of gang fights their other members have been in. In fact, researchers have said the most troubling thing about gangs' social media use is how it has sped up and amplified (made bigger) the cycle of violence. Many gang members know police can see what they post, so they tend to avoid specifics about the types of crimes they have committed, but they can use Facebook Live, Twitter, Instagram, and other apps as a form of 21st-century graffiti—promoting their own gang and disrespecting rival ones. Sadly, the *Washington Post* reported, "The online aggression can quickly translate into outbreaks of real violence—teens killing each other over emoji and virtually relayed gang signs."[57]

Additionally, social media posts are public and permanent. When two gang members exchange insults, other members of the gangs can see it and may get involved as well. Desmond Patton, a cyber banging researcher and assistant professor of social work and sociology at Columbia University, said, "These posts don't go away. You see people pulling up posts from two

Nearly everyone uses social media in the 21st century—even gang members. In addition to picking fights with rivals, they may post statuses or photos that brag about how much money they are making or how respected they are.

months ago, even a year ago, and how it can trigger conflict between gangs."[58]

In some cases, gangs use social media to try to recruit new members, but experts say these are more likely to be new, younger gangs who are desperate for more members; older, more established ones can rely on word of mouth in the neighborhood to bring new people to them. Additionally, these older gangs are more likely to use private online groups to organize and post details of criminal activity, getting the word out to their fellow gang members more quickly. Those who access gang information over the internet may be more gangster wannabes than potential gangsters. "Teens who are having difficulties fitting into a healthy group of friends may seek involvement with a gang ... and establish sites or engage in discussions that make it appear that they are gang members,"[59] said Nancy E. Willard, former director of the Center for Safe and Responsible Internet Use. The internet has not been shown to be a successful way of boosting membership in real gangs. "The gangs we deal with build their relationships on loyalty, trust and friendship," said Chuck Zeglin, a LAPD gang expert, "and there's no way of getting that on the Internet."[60] Researchers still know very little about the ways gangs use social media due to their frequent use of privacy settings, so studies in this area are ongoing.

NOT SO TOUGH?

"Two sources in particular have a tendency to misrepresent the characteristics and activities of youth gangs: the gangs themselves and the media. These are common sources of popular images of youth gangs in the United States. However, most youth gangs are not as formidable as these sources would have us believe."

—James C. Howell, gang researcher

James C. Howell, "Menacing or Mimicking? Realities of Youth Gangs," *Juvenile and Family Court Journal*, Spring 2007, p. 39.

Gangs use everything at their disposal—from movies and music to the internet and street-level recruiting—to make their lifestyle seem thrilling and enviable. They depict themselves as family-like associations with lifelong, unbreakable bonds. The reality of most gangs, however, is that the very philosophies around which they build their membership, such as brotherhood for life and putting the gang before everything else, might be mere myths that gangs do a good job of keeping alive. Gang membership is not glorious, and it is up to communities to find a better way of providing support to young adults so they do not feel the need to join a gang and find this out firsthand.

Solving the Problem

The violence and horror that frequently accompany gang crime creates strong feelings of anger and disgust in most onlookers. In 2018, for example, President Donald Trump stated, "You wouldn't believe how bad these people are. These aren't people. These are animals."[61] Due to his lack of specification about who "they" are, critics believed he was speaking about all immigrants, but he later clarified that he meant MS-13 in particular. Many people were satisfied with this explanation, but researchers say this kind of dehumanization of gang members contributes to the continuation of the problem.

MS-13 has become one of the most feared and hated gangs, not only in the United States, but in Central America as well. Many people favor harsh punishments for these gang members due to their violent actions.

OVERLOOKING THE ISSUE

"The White House put out a statement ... that described recent murders carried out by 'MS-13 animals.' Lost in the controversy over whether it was OK to call gang members animals was the fact that of the six identified victims, five were immigrants and the other was a child of immigrants."

—Hannah Dreier, journalist, on the fact that MS-13 members in the United States mostly target immigrants

Hannah Dreier, "I've Been Reporting on MS-13 for a Year. Here Are the 5 Things Trump Gets Most Wrong," ProPublica, June 25, 2018. www.propublica.org/article/ms-13-immigration-facts-what-trump-administration-gets-wrong.

Social issues such as lack of adult supervision during childhood, living in poverty with few or no good job options, the ability to make money quickly by committing crimes, schools that do a poor job of making students feel valued, and dangerous neighborhoods where young people fear for their own safety have all been shown to be underlying reasons for the appearance and growth of gangs across the country. They are things that communities may be able to do something about, but people tend to think of gangs as an issue of crime, not of society, and if gang violence flares up in a community, police are generally expected to deal with it or are blamed if gang violence gets out of hand. However, this is not a perfect solution. While it is true that specialized police forces can get gang members off the streets by arresting them, sending them to prison creates new problems. Prisons in the United States are becoming overcrowded, leading to poor conditions, human rights violations, and lack of space in which to put new prisoners. Additionally, the cost of housing and feeding prisoners is a growing burden on taxpayers. All the while, inside prison, the gang culture remains strong. "You can't arrest your way out of gang type situations,"[62] said Paul Joyce, a former police superintendent in Boston. Instead, experts say, the best way to address the gang problem is to address the factors that cause people to join, stopping gang involvement before it starts.

SOCIETY'S FAILURE

"Every society offers its members something, whether it's a sense of belonging, power, affection, status, or something else of value to the recipient. What gang researchers have discovered is that, for many children in the United States, neighborhood and community social institutions which are supposed to provide these things are not … gangs *are*. If we understand that, we can develop ways to provide these things to local youth legitimately so that joining a gang is not necessary."

–Michael K. Carlie, gang researcher

Michael K. Carlie, "The Gang Culture," Into the Abyss: A Personal Journey into the World of Street Gangs, 2002. people.missouristate.edu/michaelcarlie/what_I_learned_about/gangs/culture.htm.

The Pros and Cons of Law Enforcement Action

It is important for people who commit crimes to be punished for those crimes, especially when innocent people are hurt. However, belonging to a gang is not in itself illegal, nor can police target people for arrest just because they belong to a gang that committed a certain crime. Instead, law enforcement agencies must find specific individuals who have broken a law. Police can make arrests based only on probable cause—a reasonable belief that a specific person committed a specific crime—but they must provide evidence to back up their suspicions if that person is going to be put on trial. However, learning which gang members are responsible for crimes and arresting them can be an inefficient and time-consuming process. Many police departments have formed gang units to get to know the gangs and gang members in their communities and to deal with gang problems. This has enabled police departments to better understand criminal motivations and to make more gang arrests.

Additionally, local and national police forces conduct frequent gang sweeps, which are widespread roundups of serious gang offenders in a community. Hundreds of law enforcement officers take part in such sweeps. They approach a gang territory, taking into custody numerous gang members on whom they have collected enough evidence to get an arrest warrant. Gang sweeps can result in dozens of arrests. Although this gets criminals off the street quickly and can be an effective short-term solution,

> *law enforcement officials and analysts are divided on whether they are effective in combating gang violence in the long-term. "The gang sweep is a tool, but if that's the only tool you have in your toolbox, you're going to fail," said Richard Valdemar, who spent more than 30 years battling gangs as a member of the Los Angeles County Sheriff's Department.*[63]

New members quickly take their old leaders' place, and those who have been arrested frequently join a gang in prison or rejoin their old gang when they are released—especially when they feel they have nowhere else to go.

Law enforcement is an important aspect of the anti-gang approach, but it is much more effective in the long term when combined with other strategies.

In Chicago, police have tried to monitor current and potential future gang members by creating a gang database, which includes the names of around 130,000 people who are suspected of belonging to a gang. This seems like a good way for police to keep an eye on gangs, but in an opinion article for the *New York Times*, Tamar Manasseh explained why it is problematic:

> *Chicago's gang database has become one of the few issues that community activists and a growing number of elected officials agree is flawed and needs to be reformed. It sweeps in young people who are "likely offenders." In reality, anyone can get on the list, and for reasons like dressing a certain way, having tattoos or just sitting on their porch at the wrong moment. It's depressing but unsurprising that more than 90 percent of people in the database are black or Latino, a majority of whom have never been arrested for a violent offense or for a drug or weapons charge.*[64]

Because the perception of gang members is skewed toward people of color, they are the ones most frequently targeted by police. This leaves white gang members free to continue their illegal activities and unfairly targets people of color who have no interest in joining a gang. When the innocent people who are targeted are poor, it becomes much harder for them to fight the wrongful criminal charge because they are often unable to afford a lawyer. The stereotyping of gang members and the desire to get them off the streets, Manasseh wrote, makes ordinary citizens unconcerned with these problems: "When violence and crime are the norm, it's no wonder that a shell-shocked and struggling community will give the police carte blanche [free rein] to hunt down the 'bad guys' … If

Black and Latinx men are frequently assumed to be gang members—especially if they dress a certain way or act unfriendly—even if they have no ties to any gang.

the police say they are 'documented gang members,' fine, just get them off our streets ... If the police say that you're in a gang, you must be, right?"[65]

Another major problem researchers have noted with police response to gangs is that gang task forces rarely speak to people in the community and do not see it as their job to address the underlying social issues that contribute to gang membership. According to gang researcher Michael K. Carlie, "for police to be effective with gangs, there must be a police-community connection ... In its absence, the police are working alone and fail to obtain needed information, cooperation, and other resources available to them from most communities."[66] This disconnect between the police and the communities creates distrust of law enforcement, which contributes to making people want to join gangs. Law enforcement officers who work with the community tend to be much more successful. One example is the Unity Walk, an event organized by brothers Terry, Wilson, and Randy Riddick in areas with a high level of gang violence. They work with the FBI to set up marches; at the end of the march, the gang members can turn in their illegal guns to the FBI without fear of punishment. If they do so, they get a free haircut from one of the Riddick brothers, who are all barbers. The gang members and the police both participate because the Riddicks have built a bridge in the community, offering help and support to the gang members and getting police to listen to community concerns.

Gangs are often branded as a violent, costly, and unwanted criminal plague. However, not all gang members are criminals, and not all criminals belong to gangs. "Law enforcement officers must maintain objectivity and refrain from stereotyping gang members,"[67] wrote Kären M. Hess and Christine Hess Orthmann. Stereotyping likely only reinforces gangsters' instincts to stick together and oppose police. People should also remember that the growth of gangs is a symptom of other social issues. Focusing only on putting gang members in jail is not a long-term answer for dealing with gangs. Instead, local and national leaders must concentrate on what makes people join gangs and stay in them, then give potential and current gang members different, more positive ways to meet the needs that gangs fulfill.

Acknowledging the Problem

It is important for cities, towns, and communities to realize that the gang "problem" that leads to tragic shootings and other violence does not appear overnight. By the time gang-related violence and crime have erupted in a community, gangs generally have been present long enough for at least two different groups to establish themselves, recruit members, obtain weapons, and develop a rivalry that leads to violent public clashes. Whenever there is a rise in immigration in a country that comes around the same time as a surge in gang violence, those new immigrants tend to get blamed. However, according to researcher Amir Rostami of Stockholm University, "It takes years for migrants to be settled enough to be sucked into crime."[68] Publicly confirming that gangs exist in a community is something that should happen much earlier than it does, both to address the issue and to prevent blaming the wrong people, which makes it harder to figure out where the real problem lies.

"Failure to recognize or acknowledge the existence of gang activity ... dramatically increases a gang's ability to thrive and develop a power base," wrote Hess and Orthmann. However, among the communities they have studied, they said several "began to address gang issues only when high-profile gang-related incidents occurred."[69] By the time many communities are ready to admit to a gang problem, gangs may be deeply rooted, and a gang-related tragedy has probably happened already.

Experts—including gang researchers, most law enforcement agents, and some politicians—agree that there is no single solution to the gang problem. Police response is one necessary part of the solution, but it cannot be the only one. As the National Gang Center noted, relying too much on one particular strategy does not produce long-term, meaningful change. If gang members are arrested and sent to prison but no changes are made in the community to address poverty and joblessness, they will find themselves right back where they started when they get out. In their report about female gang members in South Africa, Shaw and Skywalker described short-, medium-, and long-term strategies that must be taken to have permanent effects on gangs.

Creating Opportunities for Former Gang Members

In the short-term, communities must focus on providing ways to help current gang members leave safely—but more importantly, they must provide reasons. For example, many people stay in gangs because they are unable to get jobs; many businesses do not want to hire former gang members—often identified by their tattoos or other markings—and most gang members did not learn the skills to succeed in the workplace when they were young. For these reasons, a community rehabilitation program to teach former gang members marketable skills may be helpful. For example, Homeboy Industries in Los Angeles is a nonprofit organization that offers free services to former gang members, including job training, employment at Homeboy Industries-owned businesses such as Homeboy Diner and Homegirl Catering, mental health services that address mental illness and substance abuse, certification in installing and maintaining solar panels (a growing industry in the United States with many available jobs), and education through a partnership with Learning

Shown here is a prison class in El Salvador attended by former members of the MS-13 and Barrio 18 gangs. The class, which is teaching them how to crochet and knit, is one of several offered by the prison's gang rehabilitation program.

Tattoos and Gangs

Most people who have tattoos are not in any gang; people frequently get tattoos because they believe they are beautiful or represent something personal and sentimental. However, while tattoos have gained more acceptance in mainstream culture in the last few decades, most people still stay away from getting them on their hands or face—areas that have traditionally marked gang involvement. Many businesses hesitate to hire employees who have tattoos in these areas or who are tattooed from head to toe.

It is not possible to make one single statement that is true of all tattoos or people who have them. Some people who are tattooed all over their body are gang members; others are not. Many people who have facial tattoos are gang members; some are not—this is a growing trend, especially among certain celebrities. In general, gang tattoos in Western societies tend to be in black and white. However, the design is more telling than the color, and many people who have black and white tattoos are not in gangs. Gang tattoos also tend to be visible all over the body and include the gang's name or symbol. These are only generalizations, though. Some people are not in gangs long enough to get more than one tattoo, or any at all, and the majority of people with tattoos have no gang affiliation.

Works Charter High School. Although Homeboy Industries is local to Los Angeles, other nonprofits are nationwide. One example is Fresh Start Removal Program, Inc., which removes visible gang and prison tattoos on the face, neck, and hands for free so people have a better chance of reducing the discrimination they face from potential employers, police officers, and the general public. According to the organization, without a job, 90 percent of former inmates return to prison; after getting a job, only 10 percent do.

Sadly, the stigma against gang members leads some people to believe that rehabilitation programs such as these are a waste

Shown here are an unidentified gang member (left) and professional French soccer player Antoine Griezmann (right). Both have tattoos, but there are clear differences between them.

of time because, they feel, gang members are monsters who cannot change their ways. However, studies have shown the opposite. One 2017 study through FIU surveyed about 1,200 current and former MS-13 members and found that nearly 70 percent want to leave the gang but do not know how because of the enduring myth, both inside and outside gangs, that gang membership is for life. Backing up former studies' findings, researchers from the FIU study reported that people can leave and create a successful life if they are given training, education, and job opportunities. According to José Miguel Cruz, the study's lead investigator, "A gang rehabilitation program run by League

The Skin Deep Project

In 2016, photographer Steven Burton started a Kickstarter campaign to promote his photography series, "Skin Deep." In this project, Burton took pictures of heavily tattooed former gang members and spent more than 400 hours removing the tattoos in Photoshop to show that without them, gang members look just like any other person. He also recorded several interviews in which he showed his subjects the Photoshopped pictures. Many became emotional in the interview; for example, one man named Marcos, looking at the two pictures side by side, said, "Man, this is art right here, man. This is a human being, a human like you, eh?"[1] Another, named Calvin, had a message for others in his position: "Don't let nobody stereotype you. You can achieve anything, you know what I mean? You just gotta put your mind to it and just keep moving forward ... To see that picture without the tattoos, I just seen it like, that was the beginning of my life."[2] Burton's goal was to humanize former gang members and show that the stigma society places on people with these types of tattoos can influence not only how former gang members are treated by society, but also how they view themselves.

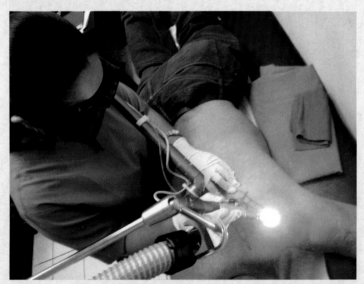

Getting a tattoo removed can be a painful process, but many former gang members feel it is worth it.

1. "Skindeep_homeboys_Kickstarter_Marcos, Im Like You Eh!," YouTube video, 0:54, posted by skindeepproject, October 22, 2016. www.youtube.com/watch?v=DPRIB8OAP98#action=share.

2. "Skindeep_homeboys_Kickstarter_Calvin–Don't Give Up," YouTube video, 1:19, posted by skindeepproject, October 22, 2016. www.youtube.com/watch?v=5tQI34em8TA#action=share.

Collegiate Outfitters in Central America has been successful … because it offers former gang members a protective environment, as well as employment, educational opportunities and tangible [real] support."[70] The results of the study could be used to shape public policy decisions both in the United States and Central America in a way that effectively targets the true causes of gang membership.

Preventing Recruitment

An important medium-term solution, according to Shaw and Skywalker, is preventing people from joining gangs in the first place. Since a major reason for gang involvement is lack of close friendships and family ties, they suggested that communities create "systems of 'belonging,'" including "a variety of programmes and activities in marginalised areas, including sports, youth groups, crafts and educational projects."[71] This would give young adults a chance to meet other people with similar interests, reducing their desire to join a gang in an effort to find love and acceptance.

School clubs offer young adults an opportunity to make friends and give them somewhere to spend time other than their house. This is important for teens who experience tension at home.

Another crucial issue that must be addressed is the problem of substance abuse. Many gang members have an addiction to drugs or alcohol—an expensive habit to support, especially without a job. In some areas, gang members that are involved in drug trafficking give drugs to young adults for free to get them interested in acquiring more, which gives business to the gang. Drug addiction is a particular issue for female gang members, since sexual assault is more likely to occur when either the victim or perpetrator—or both—are under the influence of drugs or alcohol.

One way to combine rehabilitation with prevention is to give former gang members jobs working with youth in the community. One after-school program run by Derek Brown, an ex-gang member, is called Boxing Out Negativity. Brown "teaches his students the art of boxing, checks their homework and visits their schools[;] he also warns them about rap music and how seductive the life may seem in verse, but how destructive it is when played out in real life."[72] Brown has stated that rap music played a large role in his gang involvement and noted that in addition to promoting violence and crime, it promotes use of drugs and alcohol. He told the *Chicago Tribune* that "in the absence of more positive role models, the singers take up the slack."[73] With Boxing Out Negativity, Brown hopes to become the good role model young adults who are at risk for gang involvement need.

In many places where gang activity is high, local governments unfortunately do not provide the type of social support needed to prevent people from joining gangs. For example, inner-city public schools tend to be poorly funded, which means there are fewer school-sponsored clubs and activities for young adults to join. To address this problem, basketball star LeBron James, a native of Ohio who was once an at-risk student himself, has used some of the money he makes as a professional athlete to start a public school called the I Promise School. The school, which opened in July 2018 in Akron, Ohio, includes features such as "a long school day (eight hours); a 'support circle' for students after lunch; and GED courses [high school-equivalent education for adults] and job placement for parents ... The school selected area students from among those who trail their peers by a year or two in academic performance,"[74] since this is something that increases a student's risk. Because the school day is longer, there is time for the staff to provide emotional support as well as educational classes—something many people are unable to afford, but which has a big impact on a person's quality of life. Students also receive free meals throughout the day and a free bicycle. James has promised each student who graduates that he will pay for their tuition at the University of Akron. Since it is a public school, it is mostly government-funded, but James has already contributed more than $2 million to the project. All of the school's aspects are designed to improve life for people who are living in poverty and do not have access to good education or employment options.

Basketball star LeBron James has been praised for using part of his fortune to give back to the community he grew up in by founding a public school for at-risk students.

Long-Term Social Change

Prevention strategies alone are not likely to eliminate the gang problem, but combined with rehabilitation programs and long-term policy changes, they can have a significant impact. Unfortunately, communities are sometimes criticized for spending public money in an attempt to fix people's private financial and home-life problems. For example, although one major reason why people join gangs is to make money, many people oppose government-funded welfare programs that would help people who are living in poverty pay for basic necessities such as food and housing. Because of the false perception that poverty is due to a moral failing, many politicians as well as members of the general public oppose welfare programs that would help the poor, viewing the programs as undeserved handouts. With no job opportunities and no financial help from the government, some people who are living in poverty turn to gangs to support themselves and their families.

Restructuring the welfare system and the way people living in poverty are viewed by society is not the only long-term strategy needed. Since child abuse and neglect are factors that put young people at risk of joining gangs, communities also may be able to improve family relationships by educating new parents and providing more resources, such as child care, for working parents. Communities can also work to provide more employment opportunities, better access to drug treatment facilities, and better awareness of domestic abuse as well as better protection for its victims. "Children do not choose the families into which they are born, the communities where they live, the schools they

PAYING ATTENTION TO NON-GANG MEMBERS

"The biggest cause of gangs is we do nothing for the 90 percent who aren't gang members. If all the attention and respect goes to the gang members, then what happens to the kids who aren't getting that attention and are getting beaten up by gang members?"

—Richard Valdemar, retired Los Angeles gang investigator, on why young adults join gangs for protection

Quoted in Melanie Basich, "TREXPO West: Are Gang Members Hopeless?," *Police: The Law Enforcement Magazine*, May 1, 2009 attend," James C. Howell wrote. Reducing risks of gang participation, he continued, "involves changing conditions to which youth are exposed that negatively affect their life chances."[75]

Avoiding Stereotypes

Perhaps the most vital thing society can do to diminish gang-related problems is to educate all people, gang members or not, about the realities of gang life. Too many people have misconceptions about gangs—mostly coming from what they see in the media or hear from people who do not have firsthand knowledge of gangs—and these only serve to worsen gang problems. The dehumanization of gang members and people's perception of them as "monsters" and "animals" who love fighting and killing tends to make people resist putting social measures in place to help them. If more people were aware that gang membership is largely driven by fear, they might feel differently. Once they are in a gang, most members who remain do so because they fear retaliation from the gang or rival gangs if they were to leave, and they also fear the unknown world outside the gang. Poorly educated, with no guarantee that they could find a job or a place to live, many members stay in the gang because it is the only lifestyle they know.

THE MEDIA'S RESPONSIBILITY

"Most of what Americans know about gangs is acquired through the mass media, not through personal experience … [and] what the media presents may not always be accurate … Paralyzing listeners, readers, and viewers with horror stories about gang initiations, gang fights, and gangland murders … may sell newspapers, but it doesn't solve problems. A responsible press and responsible broadcast journalism are powerful tools for bringing about change in a community by providing accurate and useful information."

–Michael K. Carlie, gang researcher

Michael K. Carlie, "The Gang Culture," Into the Abyss: A Personal Journey into the World of Street Gangs, 2002. people.missouristate.edu/MichaelCarlie/SOLUTIONS/INSTITUTIONS/what_your_local_media_could_do.htm.

If the problem of criminal gangs is ever to disappear, society must become more successful at providing good alternative ways for young people to avoid them. People also must learn to see gangs not as a curse but as institutions that, for centuries, have met the needs of certain people when society has failed them. Most gangs are signs of social problems and a result of social struggle. As hard as it may be to address gang problems, gangs themselves are a powerful force in society—one that cannot be ignored.

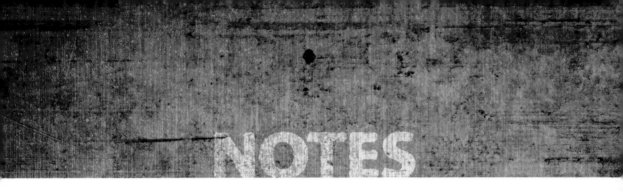

Introduction: What Is a Gang?

1. Heidi Stevens, "Gang: A Loaded Word," *Chicago Tribune*, July 27, 2011. www.chicagotribune.com/lifestyles/ct-tribu-words-work-gang-20110727-story.html.

2. "Measuring the Extent of Gang Problems," National Gang Center, accessed on August 2, 2018. www.nationalgangcenter.gov/survey-analysis/measuring-the-extent-of-gang-problems.

Chapter 1: The Rise of Gangs in the United States

3. David Kale, *The Boston Harbor Islands: A History of an Urban Wilderness*. Charleston, SC: History Press, 2007, p. 67.

4. Steven David Valdivia, *Forces … Gangs to Riots: Why and How Some Communities Erupt and How We May End It*. Raleigh, NC: LULU, 2008, p. 11.

5. Thomas Reppetto, *American Mafia: A History of Its Rise to Power*. New York, NY: Henry Holt, 2004, p. 22.

6. Reppetto, *American Mafia*, p. 18.

7. "When the Dead Rabbits and Bowery Boys Ruled Five Points," Amorq, December 12, 2017. amorq.com/article/4959/when-the-dead-rabbits-and-bowery-boys-ruled-five-points.

8. Donald J. Shoemaker, *Juvenile Delinquency*. Lanham, MD: Rowman & Littlefield, 2009, p. 260.

9. Quoted in Lee Daniels, "House of UMOJA," *Black Enterprise*, May 1981, p. 30.

10. Quoted in Dee Lockett, "Cardi B Explains the Obvious Reason She's Always Repping the Bloods," *Vulture*,

April 9, 2018. www.vulture.com/2018/04/cardi-b-confirms-why-shes-always-repping-the-bloods.html.

11. Quoted in Donna Ladd, "Dangerous, Growing, yet Unnoticed: The Rise of America's White Gangs," *Guardian*, April 5, 2018. www.theguardian.com/society/2018/apr/05/white-gangs-rise-simon-city-royals-mississippi-chicago.

Chapter 2: Underlying Issues

12. Malcolm W. Klein and Cheryl L. Maxson, *Street Gang Patterns and Policies*. New York, NY: Oxford University Press, 2006, pp. 207–208.

13. José Miguel Cruz, "Trump Is Wrong About MS-13. His Rhetoric Will Make It Worse," *Washington Post*, January 31, 2018. www.washingtonpost.com/news/posteverything/wp/2018/01/31/trump-is-wrong-about-ms-13-and-his-rhetoric-will-make-it-worse/?utm_term=.a1448e2e5b48.

14. Cruz, "Trump Is Wrong About MS-13."

15. Cruz, "Trump Is Wrong About MS-13."

16. "Race and Ethnicity: What Are Their Roles in Gang Membership?," National Institute of Justice, September 16, 2013. nij.gov/publications/changing-course/Pages/race-ethnicity.aspx.

17. Kären M. Hess, *Introduction to Law Enforcement and Criminal Justice*, 9th ed. Belmont, CA: Wadsworth, 2010, p. 317.

18. Martin Sanchez-Jankowski, *Islands in the Street: Gangs and American Urban Society*. Berkeley, CA: University of California Press, 1991, p. 39.

19. Stanley "Tookie" Williams, *Blue Rage, Black Redemption: A Memoir*. New York, NY: Touchstone, 2004, p. 14.

20. Bill Lee, "What's It Like to Be a Gang Member?," *Slate*, June 11, 2013. www.slate.com/blogs/quora/2013/06/11/gang_violence_what_it_was_like_to_be_in_gang_in_the_1960s.html.

21. Lee, "What's It Like to Be a Gang Member?"

22. Hannah Dreier, "I've Been Reporting on MS-13 for a Year. Here Are the 5 Things Trump Gets Most Wrong," ProPublica, June 25, 2018. www.propublica.org/article/ms-13-immigration-facts-what-trump-administration-gets-wrong.

23. *Understanding Youth and Gangs*, Acting Together—CURA, April 2014. www.cfseu.bc.ca/wp-content/uploads/2015/05/UnderstandingYouthAndGangs.pdf.

23. Jody Miller, "The Girls in the Gang: What We've Learned from Two Decades of Research," in *Gangs in America III*, ed. C. Ronald Huff. Thousand Oaks, CA: Sage, 2002, p. 177.

24. "National Youth Gang Survey Analysis," National Gang Center, accessed on August 7, 2018. www.nationalgangcenter.gov/Survey-Analysis/Demographics.

25. Kären M. Hess, *Juvenile Justice*, 5th ed. Belmont, CA: Wadsworth, 2004, p. 204.

26. Mark Shaw and Luke Lee Skywalker, "Gangs, Violence and the Role of Women and Girls: Emerging Themes and Policy and Programme Options Drawn from Interviews with Female Gang Members in Cape Town," The Global Initiative Against Transnational Organized Crime, March 2017, p. 1. www.unodc.org/res/cld/bibliography/gangs--violence-and-the-role-of-women-and-girls_-emerging-themes-and-policy-programme-options-drawn-from-interviews-with-female-gang-members-in-cape-town_html/tgiatoc-women-in-gangs-policy-note-1837-lo-res1.pdf.

27. Shaw and Skywalker, "Gangs, Violence and the Role of Women and Girls," p. 3.

28. Shaw and Skywalker, "Gangs, Violence and the Role of Women and Girls," p. 4.

29. Shaw and Skywalker, "Gangs, Violence and the Role of Women and Girls," p. 6.

Chapter 3: The Gang Lifestyle

30. Ian Bannon and Maria C. Correia, *The Other Half of Gender: Men's Issues in Development*. Washington, DC: World Bank, 2006, p. xxii.

31. Larry J. Siegel, *Criminology*, 10th ed. Belmont, CA: Thomson Higher Education, 2009, p. 107.

32. Arthur C. Brooks and John A. Powell, "America Can't Fix Poverty Until It Stops Hating Poor People," AEI, October 10, 2017. www.aei.org/publication/america-cant-fix-poverty-until-it-stops-hating-poor-people/.

33. Ed Grabianowski, "How Street Gangs Work," How Stuff Works, September 26, 2006. people.howstuffworks.com/street-gang2.htm.

34. "What Gangs Do," Los Angeles Police Department, accessed on August 10, 2018. www.lapdonline.org/get_informed/content_basic_view/23469.

35. "What Gangs Do," Los Angeles Police Department.

36. Quoted in "Mile High Killers," *Gangland*, Season 4, DVD, produced by Steven Feinartz and Tracy Ullman, A&E Home Video, 2009.

37. "Frequently Asked Questions about Gangs," National Gang Center, accessed on August 10, 2018. www.nationalgangcenter.gov/About/FAQ.

38. Grabianowski, "How Street Gangs Work."

39. Glenn Kessler, "Are Human-Smuggling Cartels at the U.S. Border Earning $500 Million a Year?," *Washington Post*, May 21, 2018. www.washingtonpost.com/news/fact-checker/wp/2018/05/21/are-human-smuggling-cartels-at-the-u-s-border-earning-500-million-a-year/?utm_term=.49cde6ce8b1b.

40. James C. Howell, "Youth Gang Drug Trafficking and Homicide: Policy and Program Implications," Office of Juvenile

Justice and Delinquency Prevention, accessed on August 10, 2018. www.ojjdp.gov/jjjournal/jjjournal1297/gang.html.

41. Howell, "Youth Gang Drug Trafficking."

42. Edward Burns, "Gang- and Drug-Related Homicide: Baltimore's Successful Enforcement Strategy," Bureau of Justice Assistance Bulletin, July 2003. www.ncjrs.gov/html/bja/gang/pfv.html.

43. Chris Mathers, *Crime School: Money Laundering: True Crime Meets the World of Business and Finance.* Buffalo, NY: Firefly Books, 2004, p. 42.

44. Elizabeth Kandel Englander, *Understanding Violence*, 3rd ed. Mahwah, NJ: Lawrence Erlbaum, 2007, p. 145.

45. Sanchez-Jankowski, *Islands in the Street*, p. 91.

Chapter 4: Promoting and Recruiting

46. Maria Konnikova, "Why Do We Admire Mobsters?," *New Yorker*, September 16, 2015. www.newyorker.com/science/maria-konnikova/why-do-we-admire-mobsters.

47. Alan Sepinwall, *The Revolution Was Televised: The Cops, Crooks, Slingers, and Slayers Who Changed TV Drama Forever.* New York, NY: Touchstone, 2013, pp. 76, 81.

48. Quoted in Kevin Powell, "Mama Said Knock Out," *Vibe*, September 1995, p. 93.

49. Quoted in Newsweek Staff, "Number One with a Bullet," *Newsweek*, June 30, 1991. www.newsweek.com/number-one-bullet-204074.

50. Quoted in Dan Frosch, "Colorado Police Link Rise in Violence to Music," *New York Times*, September 3, 2007. www.nytimes.com/2007/09/03/us/03hiphop.html.

51. "Kendrick Lamar Talks Album, Bloods and Crips, ASAP Rocky and More," YouTube video, 7:01, posted by *GRM Daily*, November 12, 2012. www.youtube.com/watch?v=iMX24h942nU.

52. "Why Gang Graffiti is Dangerous," LAPD Online, accessed on August 14, 2018. www.lapdonline.org/top_ten_most_wanted_gang_members/content_basic_view/23471.

53. "Perspectives on Gangs and Gang Violence," Nonprofit Risk Management Center, 2003. www.nonprofitrisk.org/resources/articles/perspectives-on-gangs-and-gang-violence/.

54. Scott H. Decker and Barrik Van Winkle, *Life in the Gang: Family, Friends, and Violence*. New York, NY: Cambridge University Press, 1996, pp. 64–65.

55. Quoted in "Mile High Killers," *Gangland*, Season 4, DVD, produced by Steven Feinartz and Tracy Ullman, A&E Home Video, 2009.

56. National Gang Intelligence Center, *National Gang Threat Assessment 2009*. Washington, DC: U.S. Department of Justice, 2009. www.justice.gov/ndic/pubs32/32146/index.htm#Contents.

57. William Wan, "How Emoji Can Kill: As Gangs Move Online, Social Media Fuel Violence," *Washington Post*, June 13, 2018. www.washingtonpost.com/news/speaking-of-science/wp/2018/06/13/how-emoji-can-kill-as-gangs-move-online-social-media-fuels-violence/?noredirect=on&utm_term=.a15ba04d0dc1.

58. Quoted in Wan, "How Emoji Can Kill."

59. Nancy E. Willard, *Cyberbullying and Cyberthreats: Responding to the Challenge of Online Social Aggression, Threats, and Distress*. Champaign, IL: Research Press, 2007, p. 66.

60. Quoted in Carrie Kirby, "Gangs.com: Crews Show Off Their Colors and Lifestyles on Web," *San Francisco Chronicle*, January 6, 2001.

Chapter 5: Solving the Problem

61. Quoted in Miriam Valverde, "In Context: Donald Trump's

Comments about Immigrants, 'Animals,'" Politifact, May 17, 2018. www.politifact.com/truth-o-meter/article/2018/may/17/context-donald-trumps-comments-about-immigrants-an/.

62. Quoted in Madison Grey, "How to Turn Around a Gang Member," *TIME*, September 2, 2009. www.time.com/time/nation/article/0,8599,1919253,00.html#ixzz0jOyAoP6q.

63. Milton J. Valencia, "Do Gang Sweeps Reduce Violence?," *Boston Globe*, March 25, 2016. www.bostonglobe.com/metro/2016/03/24/experts-debate-effectiveness-gang-raids/1t7v9RlTfxItu0PDcq1toN/story.html.

64. Tamar Manasseh, "To the Chicago Police, Any Black Kid Is in a Gang," *New York Times*, December 25, 2017. www.nytimes.com/2017/12/25/opinion/chicago-police-black-kids-gangs.html.

65. Manasseh, "To the Chicago Police, Any Black Kid Is in a Gang."

66. Michael K. Carlie, "The Gang Culture," Into the Abyss: A Personal Journey into the World of Street Gangs, 2002. people.missouristate.edu/MichaelCarlie/what_I_learned_about/POLICE/police_reponse_to_gangs.htm.

67. Kären M. Hess and Christine Hess Orthmann, *Criminal Investigation*, 9th ed., Clifton Park, NY: Delmar, 2010, p. 590.

68. "Why Are Young Men in Sweden Shooting Each Other?," *The Economist*, March 8, 2018. www.economist.com/europe/2018/03/08/why-are-young-men-in-sweden-shooting-each-other.

69. Hess and Orthmann, *Criminal Investigation*.

70. Amy Ellis, "Study on Central American Gangs Finds Rehabilitation Possible," FIU News, May 25, 2017. news.fiu.edu/2017/05/study-on-central-american-gangs-finds-rehabilitation-possible/111756.

71. Shaw and Skywalker, "Gangs, Violence and the Role of Women and Girls," p. 9.

72. Dawn M. Turner, "Ex-Gang Member Talks About Rap Music's Influence," *Chicago Tribune*, November 5, 2015. www.chicagotribune.com/news/columnists/ct-rap-music-gang-influence-turner-20151105-column.html.

73. Turner, "Ex-Gang Member Talks About Rap Music's Influence."

74. Max Zahn, "Inside LeBron James's New $8 Million Public School, Where Students Get Free Bikes, Meals, and College Tuition," *TIME*, July 31, 2018. time.com/money/5354265/lebron-james-i-promise-school-akron/.

75. James C. Howell, *Preventing and Reducing Juvenile Delinquency: A Comprehensive Framework*, 2nd ed. Thousand Oaks, CA: SAGE Publications, Inc., 2009, p. 60.

DISCUSSION QUESTIONS

Chapter 1: The Rise of Gangs in the United States

1. What kinds of issues in society might lead to the formation of gangs, and why?

2. What gangs have you heard of? What do you know about them? How accurate do you think this information is?

3. What are some similarities and differences between the gangs that were formed at different points in history?

Chapter 2: Underlying Issues

1. How do the underlying issues discussed in this chapter combine to put someone at risk for joining a gang?

2. Why are gangs considered different than other social groups that have names, uniforms, logos, and similar identifying features? Is it fair for gangs to be singled out as problem groups? Why or why not?

3. Do you think one risk factor is more important than the others? Why or why not?

Chapter 3: The Gang Lifestyle

1. Ian Bannon and Maria C. Correia stated that education provides different financial rewards for young people in middle-income groups versus young people in lower-income groups. Do you agree with this statement? Why or why not?

2. What are some ways that moneymaking gangs resemble legal businesses?

3. Did any of the information in this chapter challenge what you already knew about gangs?

Chapter 4: Promoting and Recruiting

1. Do you think you have been affected by gang references in movies, music, and video games? If so, how?

2. What restrictions, if any, do you think should be made on gang-related media? Explain your answer.

3. How much influence do you think gang-related media has on people's desire to join a gang?

Chapter 5: Solving the Problem

1. What are some things your community could do to help prevent young people from joining gangs?

2. Do you think passing certain laws would help solve the gang issue?

3. Why do you think it is hard for some communities to admit that they have a gang problem?

Big Brothers Big Sisters of America

2502 N. Rocky Point Drive, Suite 550

Tampa, FL 33607

(813) 720-8778

www.bbbs.org

> Lack of adult role models or close friends and family members can
> lead people to join gangs. To prevent this, Big Brothers Big Sisters
> of America pairs children ages 6 through 18 with an adult mentor.

Boys & Girls Club of America

1275 Peachtree Street NE

Atlanta, GA 30309

(404) 487-5700

www.bgca.org

> The Boys & Girls Club of America was founded in 1860 to give
> young people an alternative to gangs.

Council for Unity

50 Avenue X, Suite 366

Brooklyn, NY 11223

(718) 333-7270

info@councilforunity.org

councilforunity.org

> This nonprofit organization offers programs through schools,
> police departments, and prisons to teach people life skills that
> build confidence and a sense of community, making them less
> likely to want to join a gang.

Gang Resistance Education and Training (G.R.E.A.T.)
Institute for Intergovernmental Research
PO Box 12729
Tallahassee, FL 32317
(800) 726-7070
information@great-online.org
www.great-online.org

> Through the G.R.E.A.T. Program, which is available throughout the United States as well as certain places in Central America, police officers visit classrooms to educate students about gang prevention and to teach life skills young adults can use to avoid gangs and make positive choices for their future.

FOR MORE INFORMATION

Books

Friedman, Lauri S. *Dangerous Dues: What You Need to Know About Gangs*. Bloomington, MN: Capstone Press, 2009.
> This book examines what life is like from a gang member's point of view, from getting into a gang and living the gang life to getting out and moving on. It includes stories from people who have been involved in gangs.

Gifford, Clive. *Gangs*. London, UK: Evans Brothers, 2006.
> Full of quotes from gang members and photographs of the reality of gang life, this book offers different viewpoints on some of the most common questions and controversies about gangs.

Head, Honor. *How to Handle Bullying and Gangs*. Mankato, MN: Smart Apple Media, 2015.
> The author discusses strategies young adults can use when they encounter bullies or gang members.

Williams, Stanley. *Life in Prison*. San Francisco, CA: Chronicle Books, 2001.
> Stanley "Tookie" Williams, one of the founders of the Los Angeles Crips gang, wrote this book while he was on death row in a California prison. He describes his gang existence and how it turned out. As part of Williams's crusade to deter young people from gang life, his book shows the ugly realities of gangs from an insider's point of view.

Wolny, Philip. *Defeating Gangs in Your Neighborhood and Online*. New York, NY: Rosen Publishing, 2016.
> This book discusses the factors that contribute to keeping gangs active today and how people can avoid them.

Websites

Children's Safety Network: Youth Violence Prevention

www.childrenssafetynetwork.org/injury-topics/youth-violence-prevention

    This website gives statistics and information on the causes of youth violence as well as possible prevention methods.

End Gang Life

www.cfseu.bc.ca/end-gang-life

    This project, sponsored by law enforcement in the Canadian province of British Columbia, includes links to video interviews that expose the realities of life in a gang as well as a page that debunks common myths about gangs.

Gangfree.org

www.gangfree.org

    This website provides information about why people join gangs and strategies that work to address those issues. It is operated by the Gang Alternatives Program, a nonprofit organization that provides gang-alternative programs in the Los Angeles area.

Into the Abyss: A Personal Journey into the World of Street Gangs

people.missouristate.edu/MichaelCarlie/site_map.htm

    Researcher Michael K. Carlie worked closely with gangs for years, interviewing gang members as well as law enforcement agents. Combining this with what previous researchers have found out about gangs, he created this website to show the reality of gang life and explore reasonable solutions to it. Because of the violent nature of gangs, some material on the website is explicit, so readers should use discretion.

National Gang Center

www.nationalgangcenter.gov

    Funded in part by the U.S. Department of Justice, this organization provides information, resources, and tools to educate the public about gangs and help reduce gang activity using suppression, intervention, and prevention tactics.

National Institute of Justice: Gangs and Gang Crime

www.nij.gov/topics/crime/gangs/Pages/welcome.aspx

    This website includes links to topics such as gang definitions, anti-gang strategies, and gang-related research sponsored by the National Institute of Justice.

INDEX

A

American Gangster, 54
arrests, 15, 28, 38, 47–48, 50–51, 69–72, 74
Aryan Brotherhood, 29
Asia, 17–18, 20, 32
asylum, 27

B

Bandidos, 20
belonging, sense of, 7, 18, 24, 29–30, 32–33, 70, 79
biker gangs, 20–21
Black Gangster Disciples, 29
Black Spades, 18
blessed in, 52
Bloods, 18–19, 43, 55, 59, 61, 64
Bolden, Christian, 37, 39, 52
Boston, Massachusetts, 12, 50, 69
Bowery Boys, 15
Boxing Out Negativity, 80
Boyz 'n the Hood, 54
"broken home," 31
Brown, Derek, 58, 80
Burns, Edward, 48
Burton, Steven, 78

C

Canada, 34, 43
Cape Town, South Africa, 38, 46
Capone, Al, 16, 47
Cardi B, 19–20, 43
Carlie, Michael K., 70, 73, 83
Central America, 26, 28, 68, 79
Chesterton, England, 62
Chicago, Illinois, 14–15, 18, 30, 71–72
Chicago Tribune, 6, 80
child abuse, 30, 38, 82
civil rights movement, 18
Coolio, 43, 57
crime organizations, 13–14, 16–17, 26, 45–48, 53
Crips, 18, 32, 42–43, 55, 59, 61
Cruz, José Miguel, 26, 77
cyber banging, 64–65

D

Dead Rabbits, 14–15
discrimination, 24, 26, 29, 76
Dr. Dre, 55
Dreier, Hannah, 34, 69
drive-by shootings, 42, 44, 52, 55
drug addiction, 30, 36, 80
drug cartels, 28, 48–49
Drug Enforcement Administration (DEA), 48

drugs, 7–8, 11, 29–30, 34, 38, 41, 44–45, 49, 72, 80, 82

drug trafficking, 17, 24, 27, 35–36, 46, 49–50, 80

E

El Salvador, 26, 28, 62, 75

email, 53

Englander, Elizabeth Kandel, 49

F

Facebook, 65

false family claims, 27

Federal Bureau of Investigation (FBI), 48, 73

Five Points, 14

Fresh Start Removal Program, Inc., 76

G

gang colors, 33, 37, 43

gang database, 71–72

gang-related media, 8, 17, 19, 43, 52–60, 64, 66, 83

Gangs of New York, 54

gangsta rap, 10, 57–59

gang sweeps, 70–71

gender, 34–36, 38–40

Geto Boys, 10, 58

Global Initiative Against Transnational Organized Crime, 36

Godfather, The, 17, 54

graffiti, 33, 45, 60–62, 65

Grand Theft Auto: San Andreas, 56–57

Guatemala, 26

Gucci Mane, 43

H

hand signs, 33

Hells Angels, 20

Homeboy Industries, 75–76

Honduras, 26

House of Umoja, 18

Howell, Babe, 21, 25

Howell, James C., 46, 49, 66, 83

How Stuff Works, 41, 45

human smuggling, 45–46

human trafficking, 45

I

Ice Cube, 54, 57, 59

illegal activities, 6–9, 13–17, 24, 28–29, 32–34, 36–37, 41, 45–46, 49–50, 53, 56, 58, 64–66, 68–70, 72, 80

immigrants, 6, 11–15, 18–19, 24, 26–27, 40, 50, 68–69, 74

initiation, 23, 52–53, 83

Instagram, 65

I Promise School, 80–81

Irish, 11–12, 14–15, 18–19

Italians, 11–13, 18–19

J

James, LeBron, 80–81

Japan, 6, 17

Jewish, 11, 18

jobs, 12, 14, 18, 24, 37–38, 40, 48, 50, 69, 74–77, 80, 82–83

Joe Boys gang, 18
jump-in, 52

L
Lamar, Kendrick, 59–61
Latin America, 6, 26
Latin Kings, 18
law enforcement, 7, 14, 34,
    44–45, 48, 54, 70–71,
    73–74
Lee, Bill, 32
Los Angeles, California, 11,
    18, 25, 30, 32, 43, 50, 54,
    59, 71, 75–76, 82
Los Angeles Police
    Department (LAPD), 42,
    44, 61, 66
Luciano, Lucky, 16

M
Mafia, 13, 17, 47, 54–55
Manasseh, Tamar, 72–73
MC Ren, 58
Mexico, 6, 49
Mississippi Association of
    Gang Investigators, 29
Moran, Bugs, 16
MS-13, 6, 25–27, 34, 51,
    68–69, 75, 77
murder, 16, 35, 44, 47, 53,
    58, 69, 83
myths, 9, 37, 53, 67, 77

N
National Gang Center, 7–8,
    25, 30, 34, 36–37, 44, 74
National Gang Intelligence
    Center, 64

National Institute of Justice,
    29
Native Americans, 19, 25, 34,
    41
nativist gangs, 15, 20
New York City, 11–12,
    14–15, 18, 20, 34, 50
North Side Mafia, 64
Nuestra Familia, 18
N.W.A, 54–55, 58

O
Outlaws, 20

P
Patton, Desmond, 65
placas, 60
Plug Uglies, 14
poverty, 8, 10–11, 13, 18,
    24–26, 29, 40–41, 58, 69,
    74, 81–82
Prohibition, 16, 47, 53
protection money, 13, 45

R
racism, 11, 13, 18, 25–26, 29,
    58
Reebok Ventilators, 61
rehabilitation programs,
    75–77, 80–81
Reppetto, Thomas A., 14
Revolution Was Televised, The
    (Sepinwall), 56

S
San Francisco, California, 18
Scarface, 10

sex trafficking, 17, 36, 45
Shaw, Mark, 36, 74, 79
Sherlock, 17
Simon City Royals, 29–30
"Skin Deep" photography
    series, 78
skinheads, 29
Skywalker, Luke Lee, 38, 74,
    79
slums, 11–12, 18
snitch, 44
Snoop Dogg, 43
social inequality, 10, 18, 25
social media, 19, 64–67
Sopranos, The, 17, 55
South America, 18, 49
stereotyping, 72–73, 78, 83
stigma, 41, 76, 78
Straight Outta Compton, 10,
    54–55
subculture, 23
substance abuse, 8, 30, 75, 80
symbols, 23, 33, 35, 37, 60,
    62, 76
Sweden, 6, 50

T
Tango Blast, 45
tattoos, 17, 33, 35, 38, 72,
    75–78
territory, 11, 13–14, 41,
    55–56, 60, 62, 71
Texas Department of Public
    Safety (DPS), 45
theft, 7, 12, 23, 44–45, 53, 59

triads, 17
Trump, Donald, 6, 26, 68
Twitter, 65
U
Unity Walk, 73
U.S. Department of Justice, 41

V
Valdivia, Steven David, 14
vandalism, 7, 45
veterans, 20
Vice Lords, 18
video games, 52, 54, 56–57
Vietnam War, 20

W
Waka Flocka Flame, 43
Washington Post, 46, 65
welfare, 82
white supremacists, 29
Williams, Stanley "Tookie,"
    32
Wire, The, 55–56
word of mouth, 63, 66

X
Xzibit, 43

Y
yakuza, 17
YouTube, 65
Yu Li gang, 18

Z
Zeglin, Chuck, 66

ABOUT THE AUTHOR

Anna Collins has written a number of nonfiction books for young adults. She lives in Buffalo, NY, with her dog, Fitzgerald, and her husband, Jason, whom she met on a road trip across the United States. She loves coffee and refuses to write without having a full pot ready.